FALSTAFF

Borgo Press Books Translated by Frank J. Morlock

Anthony: A Play in Five Acts, by Alexandre Dumas Père
Falstaff: A Play in Four Acts, by William Shakespeare, John Dennis, William Kendrick, and Frank J. Morlock
Michael Strogoff: A Play in Five Acts, by Adolphe d'Ennery and Jules Verne
Peau de Chagrin: A Play in Five Acts, by Louis Judicis
Shylock, the Merchant of Venice: A Play in Three Acts, by Alfred de Vigny
William Shakespeare: A Play in Six Acts, by Ferdinand Dugué

FALSTAFF

A Play in Four Acts

by

William Shakespeare
John Dennis
William Kendrick
Frank J. Morlock

The Borgo Press

An Imprint of Wildside Press LLC

MMIX

Copyright © 1982, 2009 by Frank J. Morlock

All rights reserved. No part of this book may be reproduced without the expressed written consent of the author. Professionals are warned that this material, being fully protected under the copyright laws of the United States of America, and all other countries of the Berne and Universal Copyright Convention, is subject to a royalty. All rights, including all forms of performance now existing or later invented, but not limited to professional, amateur, recording, motion picture, recitation, public reading, radio, television broadcasting, DVD, and Role Playing Games, and all rights of translation into foreign languages, are expressly reserved. Particular emphasis is placed on the question of readings, and all uses of these plays by educational institutions, permission for which must be secured in advance from the author's publisher, Wildside Press, 9710 Traville Gateway Dr. #234, Rockville, MD 20850 (phone 301-762-1305). Printed in the United States of America

www.wildsidepress.com

FIRST WILDSIDE EDITION

CONTENTS

Cast of Characters 7
Preface 9

Act I 13
Act II 37
Act III 69
Act IV 124
Epilogue 173

About Frank J. Morlock 174

Dedication

To

Jean-Michel Margot

I didn't even know you when I wrote Falstaff, but this book is dedicated to you as a small token of how much I value our friendship

FALSTAFF, BY WILLIAM SHAKESPEARE *ET AL*.

CAST OF CHARACTERS

Prince Hal
Sir John Falstaff, knight
Bardolph
Pistol
Nym
Poins*
Snare*
Fang*
Hotspur*
Lord Chief Justice
Aide to the Lord Chief Justice*
Prince John, younger brother to Prince Hal*
King Henry the Fourth (played by the same actor who plays Falstaff)
Officer*
Coleville*
Page*
Mrs. Ford (Meg)
Mrs. Quickly
Doll Tearsheet
Mrs. Page
Knights, servants, rebels, etc.

Indicates that the character appears in only one or two scenes so there is a possibility of doubling.

FALSTAFF, BY WILLIAM SHAKESPEARE *ET AL*.

FALSTAFF, BY WILLIAM SHAKESPEARE ET AL.

PREFACE

The idea for this play began with the notion of unifying the Falstaff scenes in *1* and *2 Henry IV*. This concept gave way to incorporating as well, some of the Falstaff elements in the Merry Wives of Windsor.

The immediate impetus to write came after reading William Kendrick's *Falstaff's Wedding*, a post-Restoration pastiche. That play I read in late 1981. I then located another Restoration adaptation, John Dennis's *The Comical Gallant*. Dennis's play is an attempt to improve upon *The Merry Wives of Windsor*. Both these plays deserve to be better known. Having decided to play with the idea of doing my own adaptation, I then reread Shakespeare's *Henry IV* cycle and *The Merry Wives of Windsor*. Oddly enough, *Henry IV* was the first play I actually saw performed—at a tent theatre on the Charles River in the late 1950s. It was an exceptional performance; I have loved Falstaff, Hal, and Hotspur ever since.

Working as I had been at this time in amalgamating several old plays into one new play, the temptation to do a Falstaff play was too great to resist.

My first thought was to eliminate most of the historical content of the Henry IV plays in order to concentrate the action on Falstaff and the Prince. Fine as the historical material is, few on this side of the Atlantic are much interested in the dynastic politics of fourteenth-century England.

FALSTAFF, BY WILLIAM SHAKESPEARE *ET AL.*

I decided, however, to substitute an absurdist view of the various factions warring for control of the country. Thus the knights are constantly battling their way on and off stage. They are always in the background but ignored by Hal and Falstaff most of the time. They have other fish to fry.

The next point is that I soon decided that Shakespeare had whitewashed Prince Hal. In Shakespeare's view Hal is a clean-cut Prince Valiant on a slumming expedition. When I went back to the anonymous *Famous Victories of Henry V*, I found that it was very clear Hal had robbed his father's receivers, not merely Canterbury pilgrims, as Shakespeare would have it. But when caught he brazened it out, intimidated the receivers who might have appeared as witnesses against him, got himself arrested for brawling, and slapped the Lord Chief Justice in the face for refusing to release one of his gang when he was captured. The scene in the older play is very effective, and is included as Scene 5, of Act I, in this play. The only reason Shakespeare could have for omitting this scene was to tone down the misbehavior of the Prince. Shakespeare in *2 Henry IV* only alludes to the fact that the Prince was imprisoned, and obliquely at that. Accordingly, I have taken the view that Hal was what we would call a juvenile delinquent. His association with Falstaff, who is an old man who never truly outgrew his own juvenile delinquency period, becomes more explicable. Hal was a royal brat—and so I have portrayed him.

Hal eventually became a great King. This is not so surprising—many a youth has rebelled against his father only to outdo himself in pious imitation. Also, many very capable men placed in a subordinate position where they cannot occupy their talents or express their energy have turned to vicious distractions. Queen Victoria's son is a good example.

Hal also is a rather ruthless politician. I have taken the

position that his role as leader of a criminal gang prepared him well to be King. Hal understands power. Breaking with his old friends was statecraft not morality for Hal. His old friends were a liability; they could not assist him in running England; and new friends were needed.

Proceeding from this view of the King as talented but rather ignoble, it was easy to visualize him behaving slightly differently than as portrayed by Shakespeare, particularly as respects the motivation for his behavior. For example, I have always been a little troubled about the battle scene between Hotspur and the Prince. According to Shakespeare, Prince Hal kills Hotspur and Falstaff ignobly maims the body and tries to claim the deed as his own. Might it not have been the other way around? Hal, bent on glory certainly might not have hesitated to make himself look good. One need not make Falstaff particularly courageous or heroic to do this. Falstaff kills Hotspur in a cowardly way, but he gets the job done.

The remainder of the plot is basically an adaptation of the Falstaff material in *The Merry Wives of Windsor*, with some hints from the two earlier adaptations previously mentioned. I have tried to improve on these by making Mrs. Ford the secret mistress of Hal. This permits me to keep Hal center stage with Falstaff and eventually provide for their reconciliation. Though it was probably a later development historically, the practice of marrying the King's mistress to a complaisant courtier was a common practice in both France and England. It seems likely that Hal, being precocious in all things, might have anticipated this charming custom.

Finally, I borrowed the scene in which Falstaff consults a magician to make himself invulnerable from a Restoration play, *Guzman*, by Roger Boyle, the Earl of Orerry. This play about a Spanish braggart is long forgotten, but the scene is so Falstaffian that it deserves the rescue which I hope I have provided.

FALSTAFF, BY WILLIAM SHAKESPEARE *ET AL*.

Modern interest must center about the Falstaff/Prince Hal relationship. They are an "eternal couple." They go together; apart they never shine so brightly. No one either reading the original Shakespeare or this adaptation should doubt that this fat old man and his princely protégé love each other. That they are so unsuited, and that the bond is so strong, gives the relationship its dynamic tension and fascination. Shakespeare broke that bond to preserve his image of Prince Hal as the model of a Christian Prince and true Englishman. My own thought is that the friendship was never truly broken. In this connection, I think one may speculate that Shakespeare killed off Falstaff in *Henry V* less in response to the descendants of the old Castle family, than in response to his own intention of preserving or refurbishing the image of Hal. It would have been an embarrassing admission that an English King, and a great one at that, could have a soft spot in his heart for an unworthy, dishonest, old lecher. What might be excused as an excess of youth in the Prince was simply unthinkable to Shakespeare in a great King.

In conclusion, I may be accused of ruining several masterpieces to make a play not half so good as any of the originals. Let my excuse be that the temptation, whatever the result, was too great. Let others do better if they can, for I believe a new Falstaff play is needed.

—Frank J. Morlock
2007

FALSTAFF, BY WILLIAM SHAKESPEARE *ET AL.*

ACT ONE

SCENE 1

A room. To the left there is a window recessed so that a bed may be placed under it. Center a table over which Falstaff is slumped. Hal lies by the window. There is evidence of a debauch, bottles strewn around. From the window comes the sound of fighting in the street. The Prince is sprawled on the bed under the window.

Hal: What the devil have you to do with the time of day? (stirring slightly) You are so besotted with drinking sweet wine, and pissing out after supper, and sleeping upon benches after noon, that unless hours were glasses of wine, and dials the signs of whore and the blessed sun himself a fair hot wench in flame colored taffeta, I see no reason why you should be so superfluous as to demand the time of day, not I.

Falstaff: Indeed, you come near me now, Hal, for we that take purses go by the moon.

Hal: Well said.

Falstaff: Sweet wag, when thou art King, as God save thy grace—Majesty, I should say for grace you will have none—

Falstaff, by William Shakespeare *et al.*

Hal: What, no grace?

Falstaff: None. Not so much as will serve as a prologue to a hasty dinner.

Hal: Well, how then? Come, roundly, roundly.

Falstaff: When you are King, sweet wag, let not those of us that are squires of the night be called thieves: let us be Diana's foresters, gentlemen of the shade, good government men—being governed as the sea is—by our noble and chaste mistress, the Moon, under whose countenance we steal.

Hal: You speak well, and it holds well, too, for our fortune ebbs and flows like the sea, being governed—as the sea is—by the moon.

Falstaff: By the Lord, you speak true, boy,—and is not our hostess a most sweet wench?

Hal: As the honey of Hybla, my old lad of the castle.

Falstaff: What a plague do I have to do with a castle?

Hal: Why, what a pox do I have to do with my hostess of the tavern?

Falstaff: Well, you have called her to many a reckoning. I'll give you your due —you have paid all there.

Hal: Yes, and elsewhere as far as my purse would stretch, and where it would not, I have used my credit.

Falstaff: And would get none were it not apparent that

thou art heir apparent. But, Hal, I would to God you and I knew where good names are to be bought or stolen. The other day, an old nobleman berated me in the street about you, sir. But I marked him not. And yet he talked very wisely and in the street, too.

Hal: You did well, for wisdom cries out in the streets and no man regards it.

Falstaff: I must give over this life—and I will give it over: by the Lord, I'll not be damned for any King's son in Christendom.

(Hal laughs)

Oh, you have a damnable tongue and are indeed able to corrupt a saint, which the Lord be thanked, I am not. You have done much harm upon me Hal, God forgive you for it. Before I knew you, Hal, I knew nothing, and now am I little better than one of the wicked.

Hal: (slyly) Where shall we take a purse tomorrow, Jack?

Falstaff: Where you will, lad.

(Suddenly the door to the right bursts open and several knights enter fighting. Shouts of "Take that," "Have at you," "Scoundrel," "Dog," and "Puppy" are exchanged. Hal and Falstaff ignore the fighting and continue their conversation. The knights beat each other off stage out the other door. Idly, Falstaff and Hal pick up pistols and discharge them at the knights. Generally, their aim is not good. Occasionally, they wound or kill one of the knights.)

BLACKOUT

Scene 2

A forest. When the lights go up knights are fighting each other off across stage. Shouts of "Son of a bitch," "Bastard," and other modern obscenities. The knights are now dressed in more modern garb, such as Blue and Grey. As the noise of the fighting dies down, enter Hal and Poins. Poins is a big, athletic, muscular man. He plays tennis with the Prince and functions as a sort of bodyguard.

Falstaff: (shouting, off) Poins!

Hal: Stand close.

(Poins hides)

Falstaff: Poins! Poins and be hanged! Poins!

Hal: (coming forward) Peace, ye fat kidneyed rascal, what a brawling dost thou keep.

Falstaff: Where's Poins, Hal?

Hal: He has walked up to the top of the hill. I'll go seek him.

(Hal pretends to exit but hides)

Falstaff: I am accursed to rob in that rascal's company; the villain has removed my horse and tied him I know not where. Well, I doubt not but to die a fair death if I scape hanging for killing that rogue. I have foresworn his company these two and twenty years and yet I am bewitched with the rogue's company. If the rascal has not given me potions to make me love him, I'll be hanged. It could not be else. Poins! Hal! A plague upon you both! Bardolph! Pistol! I'll starve 'ere I'll rob a foot further. Four feet more by foot and I shall break wind. Eight yards on uneven ground is threescore and ten miles afoot with me, and the stony hearted villains know it well enough. A plague upon it when thieves cannot be true to one another! A plague upon you all. Give me my horse, you rogues, give me my horse and be hanged! (winded) It were as good a deed as drink to turn honest and leave these rogues—or I am the veriest varlet that ever chewed with tooth.

Hal: (appearing) Peace, ye fat guts. Lie down, lay your ear to the ground and listen.

Falstaff: Have you levers to lift me up again? 'Sblood, I'll not venture like this again for all the gold in your father's exchequer. What a devil mean ye to trick me thus? Good Prince Hal, help me to my horse, good King's son.

Hal: Out, you rogue, shall I be your 'ostler?

Falstaff: Hang yourself in your own heir apparent garters! If I am taken I'll blab all for this. If I don't have satirical ballads made on you all and sung to filthy tunes, let beer be my poison.

(Enter Bardolph, Pistol, and Nym)

Bardolph: Mask, mask. There's money of the King's coming down the hill, straight to the King's Exchequer.

Falstaff: You lie, rogue,—it's going to the King's tavern.

Hal: Gentlemen, you four meet them here in the narrow

Falstaff, by William Shakespeare *et al.*

lane: Ned Poins and I will walk lower—if they escape from you, we will take them.

Pistol: How many be there of them?

Bardolph: Some eight or ten.

Falstaff: Zounds, will they not rob us?

Hal: What, a coward, Sir Jolly Paunch?

Falstaff: We'll leave that to the proof. Now, my masters, every man to his business—

(Exit Hal and Poins who hide)

Falstaff: Now for the whoreson caterpillars—bacon fed knaves— Now.

(brandishing his sword)

BLACKOUT

(When the lights go up Falstaff, Bardolph, Pistol, and Nym are dividing their booty)

Falstaff: Come, my masters, let us share, and then to horse. If Prince Hal and Poins be not two arrant cowards, I know nothing—there's no more valor in that Poins than in a wild duck.

(Poins and Hal enter, disguised and masked)

Hal: (roaring) Your money.

(They all run, Falstaff, too, after a blow or so)

Falstaff, by William Shakespeare *et al.*

Hal: (taking the money) Got with much ease. Now, merrily to horse. Falstaff sweats to death and lards the earth as he runs. Were it not for laughing, I should pity him.

Poins: How the fat rogue roared.

Hal: If we hurry, we can beat them to the Tavern at Eastcheap. Come.

BLACKOUT

Scene 3

A room in the Boarshead Tavern, Eastcheap. Enter Hal and Poins.

Hal: I have sounded the very base string of humility. I am sworn brother to three waiters, and can call them all by their Christian names. They swear to their salvation that though I be but Prince of Wales, yet I am a king of courtesy, and no proud Jack, like Falstaff—but a lad of mettle—a good boy. I tell thee, Ned, you have lost much honor that you were not with me in this action.

Poins: (at the window) Sir John and the others are at the door.

Hal: Shall we be merry?

Poins: As merry as crickets.

Hal: Welcome, Jack—what kept you?

(Enter Falstaff, Bardolph, Pistol, and Nym)

Falstaff, by William Shakespeare *et al.*

Falstaff: A plague of all cowards, I say, and a vengeance too! Give me a cup of wine, boy! A plague of all cowards!

Hal: (to Poins) Behold a rosy-faced rogue watering his tomato face.

Falstaff: (to serving boy) You rogue, there's dregs in this wine. (drinks it anyway) There is nothing but roguery to be found in villainous man—and yet a coward is worse than villainous wine. A villainous coward— By God, there live not three good men unhanged in England, and one of them is fat and grows old— A plague of all cowards, I say.

Hal: How now, old pork barrel, what mutter you?

Falstaff: A King's son! If I do not drive you from your throne with a paper dagger I'll never wear hair on my face more. You, Prince of Wales!

Hal: Why, you whoreson roundman, what's the matter?

Falstaff: Are you not a coward? Answer me to that? And Poins there?

Poins: You fat paunch—if you call me coward, by the Lord, I'll stab ye.

Falstaff: I call thee coward? I'll see thee damned ere I would call thee coward, but I would give a thousand pounds I could run as fast as thou canst. You are straight enough in the shoulders—you care not who sees your back. Call you that backing your friends? A plague upon such backing. Give me them that will face me! Give me wine! I am a rogue if I have drunk today.

FALSTAFF, BY WILLIAM SHAKESPEARE *ET AL.*

Hal: Your lips are hardly dry from your last drink!

Falstaff: All's one for that! (drinking, wiping his lips on his sleeve) A plague of all cowards, still say I.

Hal: What's the matter, Jack?

Falstaff: The matter? There be four of us here have taken a thousand pounds this morning.

Hal: Where is it, Jack, where is it?

Falstaff: Where is it? Taken from us it is—by a hundred upon four of us.

Hal: What, a hundred, man?

Falstaff: I am a rogue if I were not at sword's point with 'em for two hours together. I have 'scaped by miracle. I am eight times thrust through the doublet, four through the hose—my buckler cut through and through—my sword hacked like a handsaw. Never fought better in my life. A plague of all cowards! Let them speak—if they speak more or less than the truth, they are villains, and the sons of darkness.

Hal: Speak—how was it?

Bardolph: We four set upon some dozen.

Falstaff: Sixteen at least my lord.

Pistol: And bound them.

Nym: No, no, they were not bound.

Falstaff, by William Shakespeare *et al.*

Falstaff: You rogue, they were bound—bound every man of them—or I am a starveling else.

Bardolph: As we were sharing, some fifty more set upon us.

Hal: What—you fought with them all?

Falstaff: All? I know not what you call all, but if I fought not with fifty of them I am a scarecrow: if there were not two or three and fifty upon poor old Jack, I am no two legged creature.

Hal: Pray God, you have not murdered some of them.

Falstaff: That's past praying for. Two! I am sure I paid two. I tell you what, Hal,—if I lie spit in my face. Call me an arrant ass. There was I—on my guard thus—(demonstrating) and four rogues drove at me.

Hal: What four? You said but two just a minute ago.

Falstaff: Four, Hal, I told you four. Paid two.

Poins: Ay, ay,—he said four.

Falstaff: These four all came at me, all abreast—thus. I took all their seven points in my shield—thus.

Hal: Seven—there were but four even now.

Poins: Ay, four.

Falstaff: Seven by these hilts, or I am a villain, else.

FALSTAFF, BY WILLIAM SHAKESPEARE *ET AL.*

Hal: Let him alone—we shall hear more.

Falstaff: Do you hear me, Hal?

Hal: Ay, and mark thee, too, Jack.

Falstaff: Do so—for it is worth listening to. These nine that I told you of.

Hal: So—two more already.

Falstaff: Their swords being broken—

Poins: Down fell their pants—

Falstaff: Began to give ground; but I followed close—seven of the eleven I paid.

Hal: Oh, monstrous! Eleven grown out of two!

Falstaff: But—as the devil would have it—three misbegotten knaves in green came at my back. It was so dark you could not see your hand.

Hal: These lies are like their father that begets them—big as pumpkins.

Falstaff: What, are you mad? Are you mad? Is not the truth the truth?

Hal: How could you know they were in green if you couldn't see your hand? Come tell us your reason.

Poins: Come, your reason, Jack, your reason.

Falstaff: What—under duress? Not for all the tortures in the world. Give you a reason under duress. If reasons were as plentiful as strawberries, I'd give no reason upon compulsion—I. But if you ask gentle, Hal, it was the moon. The moon came out from a cloud, and I saw them.

Bardolph: Ah, the moon.

Pistol: That's right—the moon.

Hal: I'll no longer endure this coward, this whale, this crusher of mattresses, this horse back cruncher—this huge hill of quavering flesh—

Falstaff: 'Sblood. You starveling, you eel skin, you dried onion, you bull's pizzle, you flounder— Oh, for breath to utter what you are like—

Hal: Well breathe a while—then to it again, but hear me speak one word.

Poins: Mark, Jack.

Hal: We two (indicating Poins) saw you four set on four of my father's receivers—tax collectors—bind them and steal all the money. Very good. Then did we two set upon you four and with a word—a bare word— frightened you from your prize—yes and have it here. And Jack you carried your guts away as nimbly as a race horse—for all your fat—and with the dexterity of a gazelle. Well now, what trick can you find out to hide from this open shame?

Poins: Come, let's hear Jack, what trick have you now?

Falstaff: At last. I wondered how long I would have to

continue before you admitted it. By the Lord, I knew you as well as he that made you. Was it for me to kill the heir apparent?

Hal: What do I hear?

Poins: He's done it.

Falstaff: Should I turn upon my true Prince? I could have slain thee easily, Hal—you don't carry your guard well— You know I am as valiant as Hercules— Could you believe that I, Jack Falstaff, would run from two mere striplings had I not recognized you? I thought you knew me better.

Hal: I'm damned!

Falstaff: Not so easy to trick an old fox, Hal.

Poins: Now he'll be telling how he tricked the Prince into admitting he was the robber.

Falstaff: I have always remarked that the guilty like to boast, Hal. You could not hold your tongue when I pretended to great valor—you must prove yours greater. Why, when I used to advise the Attorney General we caught more fellows that way. Let that be a lesson to you.

Hal: This surpasses all.

(Enter Mrs. Quickly. Mrs. Quickly is approaching a certain age but is still handsome. A little blowsy perhaps.)

Quickly: My lord Prince, there is a nobleman at the door would speak with you. He says he comes from your father.

Hal: Send him back again to my mother.

Falstaff: Shall I give him his answer?

Hal: Do, Jack.

Falstaff: I'll send him packing.

(Exit Falstaff and Quickly)

(Knights rush in and fight their way across the stage again. This time Red Coats and Blue Coats. They shout: "Caitiff," "Varlet," "Villain" and other medieval curses. [The scene may be omitted if Pistol and Bardolph and Poins, etc., usually play the knights.])

Hal: (paying no attention to the commotion) Now, gentlemen— You are lions. You run away upon instinct. You will not touch the true Prince.

Bardolph: I ran when I saw the others run, that's all.

Pistol: It was dark.

Nym: I was scared shitless.

Hal: Tell me now, how come Falstaff's sword so hacked?

Pistol: Why, he hacked it himself with his dagger, and said he would swear truth out of England but he would make you believe it was done in fight.

Nym: And persuaded us to do the like.

Bardolph: I did that I did not do these seven years: blushed to hear his monstrous devices.

Hal: With your face that were impossible.

(Enter Jack Falstaff)

Hal: Here comes lean Jack, here comes bare-bone Jack. How long is it Jack since you saw your own prick when pissing?

Falstaff: My prick, Hal? Too often. A plague of sighing and grief. It blows a man up like a bladder. There's villainous news abroad. Here was Sir John Bracy from your father; you must go to court in the morning. That same mad fellow Hotspur—and he of Wales—the magician—what a plague do you call him?

Poins: Oh, Glendower.

Falstaff: Owen, Owen Glendower, and all the Scots—all in arms against your father.

Hal: Well in this heat we shall buy maidenheads as they do nails—by the hundreds. When the gauntlet of war goes down—the skirts go up.

Falstaff: You say true. It is like we shall have good trading that way. But tell me, Hal, are you not horribly frightened? You being heir apparent. Could the world pick you but two such enemies as that fiend Hotspur and that devil Glendower. Does not your blood run cold?

Hal: Not a whit—I lack some of thy instinct.

Falstaff, by William Shakespeare *et al.*

Falstaff: (aside) My brains, I think.

(Aloud) Well, you will be horribly chid tomorrow when you come before your father. Best you practice an answer.

Hal: Do you stand for my father and examine me on the particulars of my life.

Falstaff: Shall I? Content. This chair shall be my throne, this dagger my scepter, this cup (placing it on his head) my crown. Give me wine to make my eyes look red, that it may be thought I have wept, for I must speak in passion.

Hal: Thus I kneel.

Falstaff: Here is my speech. Stand aside, nobility.

(Quickly, who came back with Falstaff, watches starstruck)

Quickly: Oh, Jesu. This is excellent sport.

Falstaff: Weep not, sweet queen, for trickling tears are vain.

Quickly: Lord, how he holds his countenance!

Falstaff: For God's sake, lords, support my tristful Queen—for tears do stop the floodgates of her eyes.

Quickly: Oh, Jesu. He does it just like an actor.

Falstaff: Peace, good tickle brain, peace. (declaiming) Harry, I marvel you dare to appear before me not so much as at the company you keep. That you are my son I take on your mother's word—and partly on my own opinion, but chiefly on a villainous trick of your eye. If then you are my son —why, being son to me are you so disgraced? Shall the son of England prove a thief and take purses? A question not to be asked? And from his father's tax collectors? (pause) There is a thing, Harry, thou hast heard of—known as mud and slime—mud and slime doth defile—so does the company thou keepest. Harry, I do not speak to thee in drink, but in tears—not in pleasure, but in passion— And yet there is a virtuous man, whom I have often noted in your company, but I know not his name.

Hal: What manner of man?

Falstaff: A good portly man of cheerful look, a pleasing eye, and a most noble carriage. Now, I remember. If that man should be lewdly given he deceives me, for, Harry, I see manliness and virtue written in his honest face. Keep him, the rest banish.

(Pistol, Bardolph, Nym and Poins groan)

Falstaff: And tell me now—varlet—tell me where have you been this month?

Hal: Why with this same virtuous man, father, taking purses, ha, ha, ha. I think we'd better switch parts. Play me, I'll play His Majesty.

Falstaff: Depose me, would you? Rebellion is it? If you play the King half so majestic, hang me up for a starved chicken.

Hal: Now, Harry, whence come you?

Falstaff, by William Shakespeare *et al.*

Falstaff: My noble father—from Eastcheap.

Hal: The complaints I have heard of you are grievous.

Falstaff: My lord, they are false.

Hal: Do you swear it, ungracious boy? Henceforth never look on me. You are violently carried away from grace. There is a devil haunts thee in the likeness of a fat, old man—a tun of man, this companion of yours. Why do you converse with that tankard, that swollen elephant, that ox, that grey iniquity—that ancient ruffian? Wherein is he good but to taste wine and swill it? Wherein neat and cleanly but to carve beef and eat it? Wherein cunning but in villainy? Wherein villainous but in all things? Wherein worthy but in nothing?

Falstaff: I would your Grace would let me understand you. What means your Grace?

Hal: That villainous, abominable old seducer—that misleader of youth—Falstaff. That old, white bearded Satan.

Falstaff: My lord, the man I know.

Hal: I know you know him.

Falstaff: There is no more harm in him than in myself. That he is old the more the pity. That he is fat is true—but conceive of him as stuffed with wit and merry jests—a plum pudding of a man.

Hal: He is a drunken whoremaster and thief.

Falstaff, by William Shakespeare *et al.*

Falstaff: That he is a whoremaster, I utterly deny. 'Tis true the wenches love him—but who could help it—he is cuddly like a toy bear. If taste in wine and food be a fault, God help the wicked! If to be old and merry be a sin, then many an ancient is damned. To be fat is to be hated. No, my good lord, banish lean Poins—banish scrawny Nym, banish red-nosed Bardolph—but for sweet Jack Falstaff, true Jack Falstaff, valiant Jack Falstaff, do not banish him thy son's company. Banish plump Jack and banish all the world.

Hal: I do, I will. 'Sdeath, if I gave such words to my father I might end in the Tower.

(A knocking at the door. Bardolph goes out and reenters running.)

Bardolph: Oh, my lord, my lord, the sheriff with a monstrous posse is at the door.

Falstaff: Out rogue. Play out the play. I have much to say in behalf of that Falstaff.

Quickly: Oh, Jesu. My lord, my lord.

Hal: Heigh, heigh, the devil rides. What's the matter?

Quickly: The sheriff wants to search the house. Pistol was recognized at Gadshill and they have tracked him here.

Falstaff: Do you hear, Hal? Best keep him out or we are all likely to be hanged.

Hal: And you are valiant by instinct! Let him come in.

(Exit Quickly)

(Pistol tries to slink into a corner, then under a table)

Hal: Hide the gold, Poins. How much is there?

Poins: A thousand pounds.

Hal: By Heaven it was a brave shew. But tell me, sirs, think you not that it was villainous of me to rob my father's receivers?

Falstaff: Why no, Hal. It was but a trick of youth.

Hal: Truly spoken. But as I am a true gentleman, I will have the half spent this night—and no one will have my man.

BLACKOUT

Scene 4

A courtroom. The Lord Chief Justice is seated at the bench. A guard with Pistol stands to the side.

Chief Justice: Jailor, bring the prisoner to the bar.

Pistol: Bring the bar to the prisoner.

Chief Justice: What is they name?

Pistol: My name was unknown when I came here and shall be when I am gone.

Chief Justice: I think we shall know it better before you go.

Officer: Do but send to the next jail, they are sure to know his name—this is not the first prison he has been in.

Pistol: And what need have you to ask if you have it in waiting?

Chief Justice: (reading) Is not your name Cutbett Cutter?

Pistol: What the devil do you ask for if you know?

Chief Justice: Why then, Cutbett Cutter, I indict you by the name of Cutbett Cutter, for robbing a receiver of the King this twentieth day of May, in the Fourteenth Year of the reign of our sovereign lord, King Henry the Fourth—upon Gadshill in Kent, and stealing in the company of three unknown confederates a thousand pounds destined for the Royal Exchequer, and lawful property of the crown.—Well, what do you say, are you guilty or not guilty?

Pistol: Not guilty, my lord.

Chief Justice: By whom will you be tried?

Pistol: By my lord, the young Prince, or by myself.

Chief Justice: You may be tried by a judge alone or by jury.

(Enter Hal, Falstaff, Poins, Nym, and Bardolph)

Hal: Come away, Pistol. What make you here? I must go about my business myself and you must stand loitering here.

Pistol: Why, my lord, they will not let me go.

Chief Justice: I am glad to see Your Grace in good health.

Hal: My lord, this is my man. I marvel you did not know him before this.

Chief Justice: (sourly) Your Grace will find small credit by acknowledging him to be your man.

Hal: Why, my lord, what has he done?

Chief Justice: He has robbed the post carrier, Your Majesty.

Hal: By himself?

Chief Justice: No, with several others. One had a horse much like Sir John Falstaff's bay mare, and another, a horse much like Your Majesty's black stallion.

Hal: How like you this? My father robbed of his money, and we robbed in our stables.

Chief Justice: We hope to learn more from this man.

Hal: On my word, I do not believe he did it.

Chief Justice: He was recognized and followed to the tavern where he was taken.

Hal: If he did it, he did it but in jest.

Chief Justice: In jest? He will be hanged in earnest.

Hal: What do you mean to do with my man?

Falstaff, by William Shakespeare *et al.*

Chief Justice: The law must pass on him according to justice—then he must be executed.

Hal: You mean to hang him? My servant?

Chief Justice: I am sorry that it falls out so.

Hal: Why, my lord, I ask you, who am I?

Chief Justice: You are the heir apparent.

Hal: And you will hang my man?

Chief Justice: I must do justice.

Hal: I must have him.

Chief Justice: I cannot my lord.

Hal: Will you not let him go?

Chief Justice: I am sorry his case is so ill.

Hal: Tush. Talk to me not of cases and precedents. Shall I have my man?

Chief Justice: I cannot, no I may not, my lord. No.

Hal: (boxing his ear) No. I say I will have him.

Falstaff: Shall I cut off his head?

Hal: Draw not your sword but get him safely out of here.

(Falstaff, Poins, and Nym menace the guard and rush out with Pistol)

Chief Justice: Well, my lord, I am content to take the blow at your hands.

Hal: If you are not, you shall have more.

Chief Justice: Who am I, my lord?

Hal: Eh? Have you forgot yourself? Why, merely a civil servant. The Lord Chief Justice of England.

Chief Justice: Striking me in this place, you greatly abuse me—not me alone but your father whose person I do in this office represent. And therefore to teach you what prerogatives mean, I commit you to Newgate prison until we have spoken with your father.

(To Officers) Take him away.

Hal: When I am King, my first work will be to appoint Jack Falstaff Lord Chief Justice. He would understand justice better than you.

BLACKOUT

CURTAIN

FALSTAFF, BY WILLIAM SHAKESPEARE *ET AL*.

ACT TWO

Several days later.

SCENE 1

The Tavern in Eastcheap. Falstaff is seated talking to Bardolph.

Falstaff: Bardolph, am I not fallen away vilely, since this last action? Do I not lose weight? Do I not dwindle? Why my skin hangs about me like an old woman's loose gown. I am withered like a prune. Well, I'll repent while I am so minded. I shall be out of heart shortly, and I shall have no new strength to repent. If I have not forgotten what the inside of a church is made of I am an acorn: the inside of a church! Company, villainous company, hath been the spoil of me.

Bardolph: Sir John, if you are so fretful you cannot live long.

Falstaff: Why there it is: come sing me a bawdy song—make me merry.

Bardolph: I can't sing.

Falstaff: I was virtuously given as any gentleman need to be; virtuous enough; swore little, diced not above seven times a week—went to a bawdy house not above once in a fortnight; paid money that I borrowed—several times, several times, lived well and in good company; and now live out of all order, out of all compass.

Bardolph: Why, you are so fat, Sir John, that you must needs be out of all compass—out of all reasonable compass, Sir John.

Falstaff: Amend your face, and I'll amend my life and figure.

Bardolph: (indignant) My face? My face does you no harm.

Falstaff: No—no, it does not. I make good use of it. I never see your face but I think on Hellfire and Satan. For there he is in his robes, burning, burning— If you were in any way given to virtue, I would swear by your face. "By this flame," I would say. But for the light in your face, you are a son of utter darkness. You are a miracle of nature—an everlasting bonfire—or there's no purchase in money. But, I thank you. You have saved me a thousand marks in torches going from tavern to tavern. I have maintained that salamander of yours with fire these two and thirty years: God reward me for it.

Bardolph: 'Sblood: would it were up your arse.

Falstaff: God a mercy! I should be sure to have a sore arse.

(Enter Mrs. Quickly)

Falstaff: How now, dame Partlet, the hen, have you enquired who picked my pocket?

Quickly: Do you think I keep thieves in my house, Sir John? The tittle of a hair was never lost in my house before.

Falstaff: You lie, hostess: Bardolph was shaved—and I'll be sworn my pocket was picked. Go to, you are a woman, go.

Quickly: Who I? God's light, I was never so called in my own house before.

Falstaff: I know you well enough.

Quickly: No, Sir John, you do not know me, Sir John. I know you, Sir John. You owe me money, and now you pick a quarrel to beguile me out of it. I bought you a dozen shirts and have never been paid.

Falstaff: Filthy hemp. I gave them to a hangman to make ropes of them.

Quickly: The finest velvet as I am a woman! You owe money here besides for your carousings.

Falstaff: He had his part of it (indicating Bardolph), let him pay.

Quickly: He! He is poor and has nothing.

Falstaff: Poor? Look on his face. Is it not rich? Let them coin his nose, let them coin his cheeks. I'll not pay a farthing. What will you make a fool of me? Shall I not take my ease in this inn but I shall have my pocket picked? I have lost a seal ring of my grandfather's worth forty marks.

Falstaff, by William Shakespeare *et al.*

Quickly: Oh, Jesu, I have heard the Prince tell you that ring was copper.

Falstaff: How? The Prince is a knave, a rascal. Forty marks, at least fifty with the way prices are rising. 'Sblood, if he were here I could find it in my heart to cudgel him. A copper.

(Enter the Prince with Poins, both in resplendent armor)

Falstaff: How now, lad? Is the wind in that quarter? Must we all march?

Hal: We march against Harry Percy and Owen Glendower at Shrewsbury.

Quickly: My lord, I pray you hear me.

Hal: What say you, Mistress Quickly? How is your husband? I love him well, he is an honest man.

Falstaff: Let her alone, Hal, and listen to me.

Hal: What's it all about, Jack?

Falstaff: The other night I fell asleep here and had my pocket picked. This house is turned bawdy house, they pick pockets.

Hal: What did you lose, Jack?

Falstaff: Three or four bonds worth forty pounds apiece, and a seal ring of my grandfather.

Hal: A trifle, some eight-penny matter.

Quickly: So I told him, my lord, and that Your Grace had said the ring was worthless. And he spoke most vilely of your Grace like the foul mouthed man he is and said he would cudgel you.

Hal: What?

Quickly: There's neither faith, truth, nor womanhood in me else.

Falstaff: There's no more faith in you than in a perjured pimp; no more truth than in a false prophet, and as for womanhood, the whore of Babylon, was a saint compared to thee. Go, you thing, go.

Quickly: (arms akimbo) What thing, what thing?

Falstaff: What thing? Why a pretty thing.

Quickly: I am no thing! I am an honest man's wife—and you are a knave for calling me so.

Falstaff: And you are a beast.

Quickly: Beast! What beast?

Falstaff: A mermaid.

Quickly: Why, a mermaid?

Falstaff: Why? Because you're neither fish nor fowl and a man doesn't know how to take you.

Quickly: You are an unjust man to say so. You know how to take me, you knave, you.

Falstaff, by William Shakespeare *et al*.

Hal: You speak true. He slanders you most grossly.

Quickly: As he does you, my lord. He says you owe him a thousand pounds.

Hal: Do I owe you a thousand pounds?

Falstaff: A thousand pounds, Hal? A million, your love is worth a million, and you owe me your love.

Quickly: My lord, he said you were a rascal and that he would cudgel you.

Falstaff: Did I, Bardolph?

Bardolph: Indeed, Sir John, you said so.

(Aside) There's for my face.

Falstaff: Only if you said my ring was copper—

Hal: I say it is copper—do you dare to be as good as your word now?

Falstaff: Why, Hal, as you are a man I dare, but as you are my lawful Prince, I fear you as the roaring lion's whelp.

Hal: The lion's whelp—why not the lion himself?

Falstaff: Do you think I fear you as your father, boy? May my belt break first.

Hal: (amused) If it should, how would your guts fall about your knees! But there's no room for faith, truth, or honesty in this bosom of yours; it is all filled up with guts and midriff. Charge an honest woman with picking your pocket? Why, you whoreson, impudent, swollen rascal. If there were anything of value in your pockets, I am a villain. Nothing but tavern reckonings, memoranda of bawdy houses, and medicine to make you long winded! Riches indeed. And yet you will stand to it, you will not pocket up your wrong! Are you not ashamed?

Falstaff: You know, Hal, in the state of innocence Adam fell—and what should poor Jack Falstaff do in these days of infamy? As I have more flesh than another man, I have more frailty. Flesh is frail, Hal, read the Bible. So it was you picked my pocket.

Hal: It was me.

Falstaff: Hostess, I forgive thee, go make ready breakfast, love thy husband, look to thy servants, cherish thy guests. You shall find me tractable to any honest reason.

(Exit Quickly with a curtsey)

Now, Hal, to the news at court: for the robbery lad, how is that answered?

Hal: Oh, my sweet ox—I must still be your good angel—the money is paid back.

Falstaff: I do not like paying back—'tis a double labor.

Hal: I am good friends with my father and may do anything.

Falstaff: Rob me the Exchequer, the first thing you do—and don't waste time.

FALSTAFF, BY WILLIAM SHAKESPEARE *ET AL.*

Bardolph: Do, my lord.

Hal: I have done almost as well. I have procured you a commission as Colonel of Infantry.

Falstaff: (pained) Couldn't you have made it cavalry?

Hal: It is fitting that a footpad should be a foot soldier.

Falstaff: Where shall I find one that can steal well? Oh, for a fine thief of the age of two and twenty or thereabouts: I am heinously unprovided. Well, you were a promising lad, Hal, I had high hopes of you, but I fear you are turning into a Prince in earnest. Well, Lord be thanked for these rebels, they offend none but the virtuous; I laud them, I praise them.

Hal: Bardolph.

Bardolph: My lord?

Hal: Bear this letter to my father; this to my lord of Westmoreland. Go, to horse, to horse, for you and I have thirty miles to ride ere dinner.

(Exit Bardolph)

Hal: Jack, meet me tomorrow in the temple hall— The land is burning— Hotspur stands on high, and either we or they must fall.

(Exit Hal)

Falstaff: Rare words! Brave words! Hostess, my breakfast. War has always stimulated my appetites—

Falstaff, by William Shakespeare *et al.*

BLACKOUT

Scene 2

A street. Enter Falstaff and Bardolph.

Falstaff: What says the doctor of my water?

Bardolph: He says the water is good healthy water, but the party that made it may have more diseases than he knows of.

Falstaff: Men of all sorts delight in making jest of me. I am not only witty in myself, I am a source of wit in other men. What said the tailor about the satin for my breeches?

Bardolph: He said you should secure him a better man than Pistol. He would not take his bond or yours; he liked not the security.

Falstaff: Let him be damned. A rascally knave to bear a gentleman in hand, and then to stand upon security! I should as soon he should put ratsbane in my mouth as offer to stop it with security. He should have sent me satin and he sends me security. May he sleep in security for he has the horn of abundance, and the lightness of his wife shines through it, though he cannot see, yet he has his own lanthorn to light him. I had almost done penitence for committing the sin of adultery with that woman! Have the aldermen provided us with sufficient recruits?

Bardolph: Here's the roll, Sir John.

Falstaff: Let me see, let me see. So, so, so, so, so— Are they good limbed fellows and strong?

Bardolph: Only one—Jack Bulldog—the rest, tailors, farmers, ragamuffins, apprentices. Very unfit for duty.

Falstaff: Too bad the tailor cannot mend them and make them fit to go. Well, we shall have this Bulldog, as for the rest—

Bardolph: I have three pounds to release Bulldog—

Falstaff: (taking half the money) Let Bulldog stand aside, we'll take the rest. Care I for the limbs, the thews, the stature, bulk and big assemblance of a man? Give me a man of spirit—let him be spare and raggedy, so he has spirit—

(Enter the Lord Chief Justice and an Aide)

Bardolph: Sire, here comes the Lord Chief Justice that committed the Prince for striking him.

Falstaff: Stand between us; I will not notice him.

Chief Justice: What's he that goes there?

Aide: Sir John Falstaff, your lordship.

Chief Justice: He that was questioned for the robbery of His Majesty's tax collectors?

Aide: The same, my lord. But nothing could be proved. As I hear he is now going as a Captain to support Prince Harry at Shrewsbury.

Chief Justice: Call him here.

Falstaff, by William Shakespeare *et al.*

Aide: Sir John Falstaff.

Falstaff: Tell him I'm deaf.

Bardolph: You must excuse him, sir, he's deaf.

Chief Justice: To the hearing of anything good. Go pluck him by the sleeve—I must speak with him.

Aide: (advancing to Falstaff who manages not to see him; plucking him by the sleeve) Sir John.

Falstaff: What—so young and begging? Are there not wars? Is there not employment? Does not the King want supporters? Do not the rebels want soldiers? It's a greater shame to beg than to be on the worse side.

Aide: Sir, you mistake me.

Falstaff: Mistake you? Why, sir, did I say you were honest? No, no,—no mistake, sir. I had lied in my throat had I said so—

Aide: Give me leave to tell you, sir, you lie in your throat if you say I am any other than an honest man.

Falstaff: Hang me, if I give you leave to tell me so. You had best take your leave.

Chief Justice: Sir John Falstaff, a word with you.

Falstaff: (in a tone intended to be menacing) My good lord! God give your lordship a good day. I am glad to see your lordship abroad. I heard your lordship was sick. I must humbly beseech your lordship to have a care of your health.

Chief Justice: Sir John, I sent to you the other day—

Falstaff: Did you so? I hear His Majesty has been discomfited by the Welsh rebels.

Chief Justice: I talk not of His Majesty. You would not come when I sent for you.

Falstaff: And I hear, moreover, his health is not of the best lately.

Chief Justice: God save him.

Falstaff: God save us all. You are close to the King, my lord.

Chief Justice: His Majesty's friend—yes.

Falstaff: And are you so well with the Prince?

Chief Justice: (uneasily) What is all this? I ask you about a legal matter. Why did you not come?

Falstaff: Why I consulted a powerful attorney—learned counsel in the laws of this land—and he advised me not to come.

Chief Justice: And who is this attorney? I'll disbar him.

Falstaff: (coolly) The Prince of Wales. As I am under arms, a soldier need not answer to the civil courts.

Chief Justice: So, so. Well, the truth is, Sir John, you live in great infamy.

Falstaff, by William Shakespeare *et al.*

Falstaff: He that wears my belt cannot live in less.

Chief Justice: Your means are slender; and your waist is great.

Falstaff: I would not have it so. I would my waist was slender and my means great.

Chief Justice: Do not rely forever on your protection from the Prince. You have misled the youthful Prince.

Falstaff: Not so. He is my master in all things.

Chief Justice: Well, you may thank your service with the Prince for gilding over your night's exploit at Gadshill.

Falstaff: (aside) That too, was service with the Prince.

(Aloud) My lord.

Chief Justice: Since all is well, keep it so. Wake not a sleeping fox.

Falstaff: To wake a wolf is as bad as to smell cold steel.

Chief Justice: What do you threaten? You, a candle—the better half burnt out?

Falstaff: You that are old, consider not the capacities of us that are young.

Chief Justice: Do you set down your name in the scrolls of youth—you that are written old with all the characters of age? Have you not a moist eye? a dry hand? a yellow cheek? a decreasing leg? an increasing belly? Is your voice not broken? your wind short? and every part of you blasted with antiquity? And you call yourself young, Sir John?!

Falstaff: My lord I was born with a white beard and something of a round belly. For my voice—I lost it singing the King's praises. To prove my youth further is needless. The truth is, I am old only in judgment and understanding.

Chief Justice: Old in sin, sir. You follow the young Prince up and down like his evil angel. Did you not incite the Prince to strike me?

Falstaff: I have chided him for that.

(Aside) I taught him to hit harder.

Chief Justice: Heaven send the Prince a better companion.

Falstaff: Heaven send the companion a better Prince. I cannot rid myself of him, he is so taken with me.

Chief Justice: The King has severed you. He sends you to my Lord of Lancaster and keeps the Prince with him.

Falstaff: And who will take care of him? Your idea, I believe. Well, I thank your pretty sweet wit for it. Pray heaven nothing happens while I am away. I would to God my name were not so terrible to the enemy. There is not a dangerous action pops up but I am thrust upon it; well I cannot last forever.

Chief Justice: You may not last as long as you might. Well, Sir John, be honest, be honest, and heaven bless your expedition.

Falstaff: Thanks, your lordship. Will your lordship lend me a thousand pounds to set me forth?

Chief Justice: Not a penny, not a penny, I know you too well.

(Enter Quickly and Fang and Snare)

Falstaff: Consider on it—I may be able to do you a service when the young Prince is King.

Quickly: Mr. Fang, have you entered the action?

Fang: It is entered.

Quickly: Will your man stand to it? Is he brave?

Fang: Snare.

Snare: Here, sir.

Fang: Snare, we must arrest Sir John Falstaff.

Snare: It may cost some of us our lives. He will stab.

Quickly: Take heed of him, he would have stabbed me in my own house. If his weapon be out he cares not what he does—he will thrust like the devil and not even spare a woman.

Fang: I care not for his thrust.

Quickly: Nor I, neither. I'll be at your elbow.

Falstaff, by William Shakespeare *et al.*

Fang: Just let me get my cuffs on him.

Quickly: I am undone by him. He's an infinite thing upon my score. A hundred pounds is a great deal for a poor woman to lose. I have borne, and borne, and borne, and have been fobbed off, fobbed off, and fobbed off.

(Seeing Sir John) There he is with that red nosed swine, Bardolph. Do your offices Mr. Fang, do your offices.

Falstaff: What's the matter?

Fang: Sir John Falstaff, I arrest you at the suit of Mrs. Quickly.

Falstaff: Away, varlets. Draw Bardolph, cut me off the villain's head—throw the quean into the channel.

Quickly: (arms akimbo) Throw me in the channel? I'll throw you in gaol! Wilt thou? Wilt thou? Bastardly rogue! Murder! Murder!

(Jumping in rage) Homosuckle villain. Homosexicidal killer. A man killer and a woman killer.

Falstaff: Keep them off Bardolph! Away fishwife.

Chief Justice: Keep the peace there! What's the matter?

Quickly: Be good to me, my lord; I beseech you, stand by me.

Chief Justice: What are you brawling here, Sir John? You should be on your way to Shrewsbury. Stand from him fellow.

Quickly: I am a poor widow of Eastcheap; and he is arrested at my suit.

Chief Justice: What is the sum?

Quickly: For all I have. He has eaten me out of house and home.

Falstaff: Nonsense. And she lives with a man, and calls him husband.

Quickly: I shall have it back again or I will ride thee at nights like the mare.

Falstaff: So you would be riding? I am as like to ride this mare if I have any vantage ground to get up.

Chief Justice: Are you not ashamed, Sir John, to force a poor widow to so rough a course to enforce her own?

Falstaff: What is the sum—the gross sum—that you say I owe you?

Quickly: Yourself and your money too.

Falstaff: This does not lie at law.

Quickly: Did you not swear to me on the breast of a turkey and a hogshead of beer—the same day the Prince broke your head for kissing his whore— did you not swear to me then—as I was washing your wound—to marry me and make me your lady? Did not Doll Tearsheet come in that very moment to borrow vinegar, and did you not desire to eat some shrimp—and after she left did you not tell me to keep my distance from her—not to be too familiar with her as she is a whore, for soon ere long the people would call me madam? Deny it if you dare! And did you not kiss me, and ask me to bring you thirty shillings?

Falstaff: But you had a husband, madam? Do you deny that, or do you admit you are an infamous woman? Can a man not have a little jest, but you must take him to law? It's obvious she's mad. Poverty has distracted her.

Chief Justice: Sir John, Sir John, I know your ways. You have practiced upon this poor innocent woman—

Falstaff: Innocent!

Chief Justice: And made her serve you both in purse and in person.

Quickly: Yes, he has practiced upon me, practiced upon me, my lord, practiced.

Chief Justice: Pay her the debt you owe her, and undo the villainy you have done her.

Falstaff: I say to you deliver me from these officers— I am on the King's affairs. Do it, or look to it.

Chief Justice: You have the power to wrong this woman, and I am powerless to stop you—but clear your reputation—satisfy her.

Falstaff: (aside) That's more than I or any man can do.

(Aloud) Come hither, hostess.

Falstaff: (to Quickly) As I am a gentleman—

Quickly: You've said that before.

Falstaff: When these wars are done

(Aside) may they last forever—

(Aloud) I'll marry thee. But mark, you must get rid of your husband.

Quickly: Oh, he's just by the way. Not a real church made husband. He shall go.

Falstaff: Come—no more words on it.

Quickly: I'll have to pawn all my glasses.

Falstaff: Tush. If it were not for these humors, there were not a better wench in England. Come wash thy face and withdraw thy action. You must not be in this humor with me, come. I know someone put you up to this.

Quickly: (mollified) Give me twenty pounds.

Falstaff: Here's ten from the King's Exchequer.

Chief Justice: Are you content?

Quickly: I withdraw my action.

Falstaff: Then it's on to Shrewsbury and victory.

BLACKOUT

SCENE 3

Roadway in open country near Shrewsbury.

Falstaff, by William Shakespeare *et al*.

Enter Falstaff and Bardolph.

Falstaff: Bardolph, get thee before to Shrewsbury; fill me a bottle of sack. Our soldiers shall march through. We'll to Shrewsbury before night.

Bardolph: Will you give me money, Captain?

Falstaff: Use your own money. What don't you trust me?

Bardolph: This bottle brings it to a crown.

Falstaff: And if it does, take one for your labor—and if it make twenty—take them all—out of the company expense fund, mind you. Bid Lieutenant Pistol meet me at the town's end.

Bardolph: I will, sir. Farewell.

(Exit Bardolph)

Falstaff: (seated) If I be not ashamed of my soldiers I am a skinny minnow. I have used the King's power to draft and impress most damnably. In exchange for a hundred and fifty soldiers, I have extorted three hundred pounds. I draft none but the richest, and let them buy off and substitute the worst rabble—such as fear the sound of gunshot worse than wild ducks and partridges. Thus my whole battalion consists of derelicts as ragged as Lazarus—and such indeed as were never soldiers but discarded serving men, starvelings and unemployed apprentices. They would as lief hear the devil as a war drum. A hundred and fifty prodigals lately come from swine keeping—from eating draff and husks. A mad fellow met us marching on the way, and told me I had unloaded all the gibbets and pressed the dead. No eye has seen such scarecrows. I'll not march through Shrewsbury with them, that's flat. There's not a shirt and a half in all my company—and those stolen. But that's all one—they'll find linen enough for winding sheets. Well, Hal, I hope your other captains have served you better than I or you're likely to have a sad day of it if it comes to a battle. The noise of a cannon would knock these over.

(Enter Hal and his brother, Prince John)

Hal: How now, Jack, blown?

Falstaff: What, Hal! Mad wag—what a devil are you doing here? Good Lord, Prince John, I thought you had already been at Shrewsbury.

Prince John: 'Tis more than time that I were there—we must march all night. The King looks for us all.

Hal: I do not need your instruction, little brother.

Falstaff: Tut, never fear me. I am as vigilant as a cat to steal cream.

Prince John: And as like.

Hal: Your thefts have already made you butter—but tell me, Jack, whose fellows are those that come behind?

Falstaff: Mine, Hal, mine.

Hal: I have never seen such a pitiful rabble.

Falstaff: I have an eye, Hal, for courage. Trust my eye,

Falstaff, by William Shakespeare *et al.*

Hal. They are very fit.

Hal: Fit for cannon fodder.

Falstaff: They'll fill a pit as well as better men; tush man, mortal men, mortal men.

Prince John: But exceedingly poor and base.

Hal: And beggarly.

Falstaff: They are hungry. And hungry men fight well. Trust me for that. For their poverty, I cannot answer—and for their bareness—they never learned that of me.

Hal: I'll be sworn.

Falstaff: But don't doubt they will perform well. They have a hearty commander.

Hal: But make haste, Jack. Hotspur and Glendower are already in the field.

Falstaff: What, is the King encamped?

Prince John: He is, Sir John. I fear we shall stay too long.

(Exit Prince John)

Hal: Little brat.

Falstaff: Hal, if you see me down in battle—bestride me, so; 'tis a point of friendship.

Hal: Nothing but a colossus can do you that friendship. Say your prayers and farewell.

Falstaff, by William Shakespeare *et al.*

Falstaff: I would it were bedtime, Hal, and all well.

Hal: Why, we all owe God a death.

Falstaff: But the debt is not due yet—and I am loath to pay a bill before it is due. What need I be so forward with him that calls not on me.

Hal: God be with you, old man.

(Exit Hal)

Falstaff: Well, no matter. Honor pricks me on. But will honor prick me off? Can honor set a leg? No. Or an arm? No. Or take away the ache of a wound? No. Honor has no skill in surgery then? No. What is honor? A word. Who has it? He that died Wednesday. Does he feel it? No. 'Tis insensible then? Yes—to the dead. But will it not live with the living? No. Why? Detraction will not suffer it. Therefore, I'll none of it. Honor is a mere funeral oration. So, old man, you'd best think how to come out of this in one thick piece—with or without honor.

BLACKOUT

SCENE 4

The Battlefield at Shrewsbury. Knights battle each other on and off stage. After a moment, Coleville and Falstaff enter from opposite sides of the stage.

Falstaff: What's your name, sir? Of what condition are you, and of what place?

Coleville: I am a knight, sir, and my name is Coleville of the Dale.

Falstaff: Well then, Coleville is your name, a knight is your degree, and your place, the dale. Coleville shall be still your name, a traitor your degree, and the dungeon your place—or a place deep enough—so you shall still be Coleville of the Dale.

Coleville: Are not you Sir John Falstaff?

Falstaff: As good a man as he. Do you yield or must I sweat for you? If I do sweat, they are the tears of thy friends weeping for thy death. Therefore, rouse up fear and trembling.

Coleville: (surrendering his sword) I yield—

Falstaff: I have a whole school of tongues in this belly of mine—and not one of 'em all speaks any other name than valiant Jack Falstaff.

(Enter Prince John)

Prince John: Now Falstaff, where have you been all this while? When all is over you come. These tardy tricks of yours may yet break some feeble gallows.

Falstaff: Is this the reward of valor? Do you think me a shadow—an arrow or a bullet? Have I the speed of thought? I have sped hither with the expedition of a swallow. And here, faint from my journey, after a furious engagement, I have taken—in my pure and immaculate valor—Sir John Coleville of the Dale—a notorious and valiant traitor? But what of that? I came, I sweat, I conquered.

Falstaff, by William Shakespeare *et al.*

Prince John: More out of his weakness than your valor, I think—

Falstaff: (modestly) I know not. Here he is, and here I yield him. And I insist it be recorded with the rest of the day's deeds. Let me have justice done and merit mount.

Prince John: (amused) Yours is too heavy to mount.

Falstaff: Then let it shine.

Prince John: It is too thick to shine.

Falstaff: Call it what you will so it does me good.

Prince John: Is your name Coleville?

Falstaff: A famous rebel, are you?

Coleville: I am the same as my betters. Had they been ruled by me, they would have sold themselves dearer.

Falstaff: They sold themselves, but you like a kind fellow gave yourself gratis.

Prince John: (to an Officer) Conduct this man under heavy guard to the internment center.

(Low) To the nearest convenient tree and hang him.

(Exit Coleville and Officer)

Falstaff: When I come to court stand me good in your report—

Falstaff, by William Shakespeare *et al.*

Prince John: Fare you well, Falstaff— I shall speak you better than you deserve.

(Exit Prince John)

Falstaff: I would you had but the wit. This sober young Prince does not love me. A man cannot make him laugh—but that's no wonder, Prince Proud Lips drinks no wine. He would be King, I think. God save merry England.

(Another alarum; knights beat each other on, then off stage. Falstaff drops out of sight then sees the body of Sir Walter Blunt.)

Falstaff: Though I could escape shot free a reckoning in London, I fear the shot here. Here's no reckoning but upon the pate! Soft, (seeing the body) who are you? Sir Walter Blunt—there's honor for you! Here's no vanity. I am as hot as molten lead. (wipes his brow) God keep the lead out of me. I need no more weight— Well, I have led my ragamuffins where they were peppered. There's not three of my three hundred and fifty left alive—and they are for the town's end, to beg during life. But who comes here?

Hal: (entering) What, stand idle here? Lend me your sword— Many a nobleman lies stark and stiff under the hoofs of vaunting enemies whose deaths are yet unavenged. Lend me your sword.

Falstaff: Oh, Hal—give me leave to breathe awhile. Hercules never did such deeds in arms as I have done this day; I have paid Hotspur, I have made him sure.

Hal: He is indeed; and living to kill thee. Lend me your sword.

Falstaff: Before God, Hal, if Hotspur is alive you get not my sword. I thought sure I had killed the scoundrel. But take my pistol.

Hal: Give it me: what is it in its case?

Falstaff: Hal, 'tis hot, 'tis hot—there's that will sack a city.

(He draws it out and finds it to be a wine bottle)

Hal: What is it a time to jest and dally now?

(Throws the bottle at him)

Falstaff: Here, take Sir Walter Blunt's pistol, he has no need of it.

Hal: That's some use.

(Exit Hal)

Falstaff: Well, if Hotspur be alive, I'll pierce him—if he come in my way. If not—if I come in his willingly let him make a Turkish shish kebab of Falstaff. I like not such grinning honor as this one has. (touching Blunt's body with his foot) Give me life, which if I can save— so. (drinks from his wine bottle) If not, and honor comes unlooked for— why, there's an end. (drinks again)

(Enter Hotspur)

Hotspur: Bold Jack Falstaff, is it not?

Falstaff, by William Shakespeare *et al.*

Falstaff: Oh, shit! Ay, Jack Falstaff—and you are—

Hotspur: Harry Percy—called Hotspur because of my temper.

Falstaff: Good afternoon. Nice day.

Hotspur: Will you surrender?

Falstaff: Why should I do that?

Hotspur: I have read your fortune. You are to be the friend of a King.

Falstaff: Likely enough. I am friend to a King's son.

Hotspur: Be my friend Jack, for before this day is ended I shall be King, and Harry Monmouth, your darling Hal, shall be dust.

Falstaff: How do you prove that?

Hotspur: At my nativity, the front of heaven was full of fiery shapes, of shooting stars, and at my birth, the frame and huge foundation of the earth shaked like a coward.

Falstaff: Do you say so? Why so it would have done if your mother's cat had kittened and you yourself never been born.

Hotspur: (furious) I say the earth did shake when I was born.

Falstaff: And I say, the earth was not of my mind, if you suppose as fearing you, it shook.

Hotspur: (in growing rage) The heavens were all on fire—the goats ran from the mountains—these and other signs have marked me extraordinary. I can call spirits from the vasty deep—

Falstaff: Why so can I or any man—but will they come when you call them?

Hotspur: Very well. No more of this unprofitable chat. I spoke you fair. On your guard.

Falstaff: If ever I desert Hal for such a thing as you may I be a ham cutlet—

Hotspur: You shall shortly be sliced pork—

(They fight and Falstaff falls as if dead. Enter Hal, who sees Falstaff.)

Hal: Well, old acquaintance, could not all this flesh keep you in a little life? Poor Jack, farewell. I could have better spared a better man.

Hotspur: If I mistake not, you are Harry Monmouth.

Hal: Do you imagine I will deny my name?

Hotspur: My name is Harry Percy—

Hal: Why, then I see a very valiant rebel of the name. I am the Prince of Wales, and think not, Percy, to share with me in glory any more; two stars keep not their motion in one sphere. Nor can one England brook a double reign of Harry Percy and the Prince of Wales.

Hotspur: Nor shall it, Harry—for the hour is come to end the one of us—

Hal: I'll crop thy crest to make a garland for my head.

Hotspur: I can no longer brook your vanities—

(They fight, Hotspur is winning. Hal loses his sword.)

Hotspur: (his sword is at Hal's throat) You had better stuck to tavern brawls. Prepare yourself.

Hal: (trembling) This wasn't in the script. I'm not supposed to die. I'm the Prince of Wales—God protects me.

(To Hotspur) You cannot kill me. You have no right.

Hotspur: (ready to deliver the death blow) Might makes right. Adieu, sweet Prince—

Hal: This absolutely cannot happen.

(Falstaff has risen and taking a gun from his pocket shoots Hotspur in the back)

Hotspur: Oh, some coward has robbed me of my youth. Percy you are dust and food for— (dies)

Falstaff: For worms, brave Percy. Ambition, how much art thou shrunk.

Hal: But Jack, I thought you dead.

Falstaff: 'Sblood, 'twas time to counterfeit or that hot termagant had paid me out. Counterfeit, I lie, I am no counterfeit: to die is to be counterfeit of a man. But to counterfeit dying is to live—so no counterfeit. The better part of valor is discretion—in which part I have saved my life and yours too.

Hal: Zounds, I am afraid of this gunpowder Percy though he be dead. How if he should counterfeit and rise. I'll make him sure— (stabs Percy several times)

Falstaff: Sometimes it takes an old coward to save a young hero.

(Enter Prince John)

Prince John: (with evident disappointment) Are you alive, brother, and you too, fat knight?

Hal: Surely he is alive, though I saw him dead on the ground.

Falstaff: (kicking Percy) Jack Falstaff at your service. If your father will do me the honor, so—if not, let him kill the next Hotspur himself. I look to be either an Earl or a Duke, I can assure you.

Hal: Why, I killed him myself while you lay dead.

Falstaff: Did you? Lord, Lord, how this world is given to lying! I grant you I was down, but did I not rise up? If I may be believed, so; if not let them that should reward valor bear the sin upon their own heads. (exit Jack) I must do more wonders.

Prince John: This is the strangest tale I ever heard.

Falstaff, by William Shakespeare *et al.*

Hal: This is the strangest fellow. The trumpet sounds retreat. The day is ours—

Prince John: Let us go.

Hal: You go on ahead. I must do something here.

(Exit Prince John)

(Enter Bardolph)

Bardolph: Save you, Prince.

Hal: Just the man I need. You must help me sew up the back of Hotspur's cloak. No one must know he was shot in the back. Oh, and another thing, I shall need to change trousers with you, Bardolph.

BLACKOUT

CURTAIN

FALSTAFF, BY WILLIAM SHAKESPEARE *ET AL.*

ACT THREE

SCENE 1

The tavern in Eastcheap. Falstaff, Bardolph, Pistol, Nym.

Falstaff: (looking at his purse) My purse is near empty. I can get no remedy against this consumption of the purse. The disease is incurable.

Pistol: The army is discharged.

Nym: Take a purse.

Falstaff: I am off that game. The Prince will not do it anymore. He promised his father. And I scorn to take a purse in any but royal company.

Bardolph: We are almost out at the heels.

Pistol: What remedy? Young ravens must eat.

Falstaff: If I can't steal, I must shift. Do any of you know Master Ford, the wine merchant?

Pistol: I know the mortal, he is of substance good.

Falstaff: Honest lads, I will tell you what I am about.

Falstaff, by William Shakespeare *et al.*

Pistol: Two yards and more.

Falstaff: No quips, Pistol, no quips. Indeed, I am in the waist two yards at least. But now I am about no waste. I'm about thrift. Briefly, I do mean to make love to Ford's wife, Mistress Meg.

Bardolph: I hear some rich man is her secret lover.

Nym: Ford is very jealous, but the wanton wench is too clever for him.

Falstaff: So much the better. Briefly, I do mean to make love to Ford's wife. I spy entertainment in her eye and in her very motion she gives the leer of invitation—which translated to plain English says, Sir John, come lie with me.

Pistol: Admirably translated!

Nym: Well construed. Well Englished.

Falstaff: Now the report goes she rules her husband's purse, and he is rich.

Pistol: To her boy, I say. Halloo, old dragon, I say.

Falstaff: I have writ me here a letter to her and another to Doll Tearsheet (who though a whore, has plenty of money). Doll has given me good eyes, examined my parts most judiciously—sometimes the beam of her glance gilded my foot—sometimes my portly belly.

Pistol: Then did the sun on dunghill shine.

Falstaff, by William Shakespeare *et al.*

Nym: I thank you for that—

Falstaff: Oh, she did course over my exteriors with such a greedy appetite that I scorched. Here's another letter to her. I will be cheater to them both. And they shall be exchequers to me. They shall be my East and West Indies and I shall trade in both ports.

Bardolph: But ain't two more than an old—I mean senior citizen like you can handle?

Falstaff: Tut, old. Don't I still manage a whore every night? Old. A man's not old till he can't do it but once a week. Go Pistol to Mrs. Ford with this letter. Nym to Doll. We will thrive, lads, we will thrive.

Pistol: Am I to be your pimp? Your Pandarus of Troy? And by my side wear steel. Then Devil take all.

Nym: Nor I. I will keep up regulation.

Falstaff: Why you rogues—hence avant, vanish like hailstones, go trudge, plod o' way o' the hoof, seek shelter, pack, trot, discard. Falstaff will learn the honor of the age and rid himself of employees that strike. Fare ye well, ye brace of drills, you.

Nym: What, without money knight?

Pistol: Lend us money to subsist then.

Falstaff: I will not lend you a penny.

Pistol: Why then the world's my oyster which I with sword will open.

Falstaff, by William Shakespeare *et al*.

Falstaff: Not a penny. I have been content, sirs, you should pawn my acquaintance. I have grated upon my good friends to procure three reprieves for you and your coach fellow Nym—or else you had looked through bars like Barbary apes. I am damned to Hell for swearing to gentlemen, my friends, you were good soldiers and stout fellows; and when Lady Warwick lost her diamond, I took it upon my honor that you had it not.

Pistol: And did you not share?

Falstaff: Reason, you rogue, reason. Do you think I'll endanger my soul gratis? In one word—I am no gallows bird for you. Go. You'll not bear a letter for me you rogue? You stand upon honor? Honor? I, I, I, myself, sometimes leaving the fear of heaven and hiding my honor in my necessity am fain to shuffle, to hedge, and to lurch; and yet you, you rogue will ensconce your rages, your mangy whiskers, your alehouse oaths, and your bawdy blusterings, under the shelter of honor! You will not do it, you?

Pistol: I do relent and repent. What more do you want?

Falstaff: Very well. If you repent sincerely, I like a good friar will give you absolution. Now lads, to arms.

(Exeunt all)

(A short pause, then Hal and Poins come in)

Hal: Before God, I am exceeding weary, Poins.

Poins: I had thought weariness durst not have attacked one of so high blood.

Falstaff, by William Shakespeare *et al*.

Hal: It does me, though it discolors the complexion of my greatness to admit it. Does it not show vilely in me to desire small beer, cheap wine, and low company? Belike my appetite was not princely got. What a disgrace it is to me to remember your name.

Poins: How ill it becomes you, after all you have labored so hard, to talk so idly. How many good princes would do so, their father being so sick as yours at this time?

Hal: By this hand, you think me for deep in the Devil's book. Well, let the end try the man. I tell you my heart bleeds inwardly that my father is so sick. But keeping company with such wild company as you prevents me from showing my true feelings of sorrow.

Poins: The reason?

Hal: What would you think of me if I should weep?

Poins: I should think you a most princely hypocrite.

Hal: It would be every man's thought—and you are a lucky fellow to think always as the world thinks. What induces you to think so?

Poins: Why because you have been so lewd, and so much engrafted to Falstaff.

Hal: And to thee.

Poins: By this light, I am well spoken of: don't link my name with Falstaff's. By the Mass, here comes Pistol.

(Enter Pistol)

Falstaff, by William Shakespeare *et al.*

Pistol: God save your Grace.

Hal: And yours, most noble Pistol. And how does Falstaff? Why is he not here?

Pistol: Well my lord, he heard of your coming to town. There's a letter for you.

Hal: Humph! I do not allow this old seducer to be as familiar with me as with my dog. He stands on his rank. Look you how he writes—John Falstaff, Knight, "to the son of the King, nearest his father, Harry Monmouth, Prince of Wales—greetings."

Poins: Why this is rare.

Hal: Peace!—"I will imitate the noble Romans for brevity. I commend me to thee, I commend thee. Be not too familiar with Poins, for he misuses thy favors much and gives out you have married his sister. Confess your sins as I do and so farewell." Signed: "Jack Falstaff—with my familiars, Sir John with all England, Europe, and Asia."

Poins: I'll make him eat it.

Hal: So I am married to your sister, Ned, eh?

Poins: I only said that because people say you lie with her. I would have her thought honest.

Hal: The Devil. Must a whore be the Queen of England?

(To Pistol) Is your master back in London?

Pistol: Yes, my lord, he arrived this morning.

Hal: Where does he stay?

Pistol: Here, at the old place.

Hal: Any woman with him?

Pistol: Only Mrs. Quickly and Doll Tearsheet. But he has a design upon Mrs. Ford.

Hal: (stunned) Mrs. Ford? Old Ford's wife?

Pistol: Yes, my lord. He has disgraced me by making me carry a pimping letter to her.

Hal: Do not tell him, I am come back yet. No words to your master.

Pistol: I have no tongue.

(Exit Pistol)

Hal: What Falstaff make love to Mistress Ford?

Poins: You shall be a cuckold by proxy, my lord.

Hal: Damnation.

Poins: Jack does not know you keep her. It is a secret from him and all the rest.

Hal: What, Meg false?

Poins: All women are weak vessels.

Hal: I cannot bear this.

Poins: Tell him not to poach.

Hal: No, that would be unprincely. I value her love only as it is freely given. Let him take he if he can.

Poins: She will probably have nothing to do with him.

Hal: Yes, I believe her true. But it is well I put her to the test.

Poins: Never believe him. He will say he slept with her if he did or no.

Hal: She must have given him some encouragement. He'd never venture else—

Poins: The old fool thinks he's irresistible.

Hal: Incite Ford. Whisper in his ear, his wife has an admirer.

Poins: I will my lord.

Hal: How can we come at Falstaff, without his knowing we are about?

Poins: Persuade Quickly to hide us behind the curtains, disguised as waiters.

Hal: Good, I like the design. To your work.

Poins: Yes, my lord.

(Exit Poins)

Falstaff, by William Shakespeare *et al.*

Hal: She is false to her husband with me, why may she not be false to me? Bah! I do not misdoubt Meg—yet nor am I too confident neither. She is older than I. Still. She was in his company—and what she made there I know not. Meg dares not know me in public— Still, I am not jealous. I will look further into it. Bah, he is old. Yet, her husband is old, and belike, she likes an older man. Still, he's fat. Yet some women do not scorn a well larded man. I shall go mad. If I find her honest, I lose not my labor. If she be otherwise 'tis a labor well bestowed.

BLACKOUT

Scene 2

When the lights go up, Mrs. Quickly leads in Doll Tearsheet. Doll is a resplendent whore. Several of her lovers have recently died in the civil war and left her money. She is, for the moment very fine. Doll and Mrs. Quickly have been drinking. The scene does not change.

Quickly: Faith, sweetheart, methinks you are in an excellent good temperality. Your pulsage beats as extraordinary as heart would desire—and your color is as red as any rose. But you have drunk too much wine. How do you now?

Doll: Better than I was—hem!

Quickly: Why that's well said—a good heart's worth gold.

Doll: It's because of my heart that I've got all this gold. I was good to so many of the soldiers and three of them was so good—because I was so good hearted to 'em, that they left me legacies in their will—after they was kind enough to get killed in the wars.

Quickly: Why how much have you got, Doll?

Doll: Near two thousand pounds.

Quickly: What it is to be a lady. I am glad of your acquaintance. Why, here comes Sir John.

(Enter Falstaff and Bardolph)

Falstaff: How does Mrs. Doll?

Doll: Sick of a calm—

Falstaff: So is all your sex,—once calm they are sick.

Doll: A pox dam you, you muddy rascal. Is that all the comfort you give me?

Falstaff: You make fat rascals, Mrs. Doll.

Doll: I make 'em? Gluttony and disease makes them—not I.

Falstaff: The cooks help to make the glutton—you help to make the diseases, Doll. We catch you, Doll—we catch you.

Doll: Yes, sweetheart, you steal our pearls of chastity.

Falstaff: Pearls—half penny marbles.

Doll: Hang yourself you dirty tongue whale, hang yourself.

Falstaff, by William Shakespeare *et al.*

Quickly: You two never meet but you fall to some discord. You cannot bear one another's infirmities. You being the weaker vessel, Doll, must bear—

Doll: Can a weak vessel bear such a full hogshead? A ship's hold was never so full. Come, I'll be friends with thee, Jack, thou art going to the wars, and whether I shall ever see thee again, there's nobody cares. (weeps drunkenly)

(Enter Servant)

Servant: Sir, Lieutenant Pistol is below and would speak with you.

Doll: Hang him, swaggering rascal. Let him not come up. It is the most foul mouthed rogue in England.

Quickly: If he swaggers, let him not come here. I must live among my neighbors. Shut the door, there comes no swaggerers here. I have not lived this while to have swaggerers.

Falstaff: Let him in, do you hear.

Quickly: Pacify yourself, Sir John. There come no swaggerers here.

Falstaff: Let him in. He is my non-com.

Quickly: Fiddle-faddle, Sir John. Never tell me. I was before Justice Shallow the other day, and he said to me—it was no longer ago than Wednesday last—you are an honest woman—have a care of guests you receive. Receive no swaggerers. No swaggerers.

FALSTAFF, BY WILLIAM SHAKESPEARE *ET AL.*

Falstaff: He's no swagger—a tame card sharp. You may beat him like a puppy and he will not swagger with a Barbary hen.

Quickly: I will bar no honest man my house. Let him in. I hate swaggerers.

(Exit Servant, enter Pistol, drunk)

Pistol: God save you, Sir John.

Falstaff: Welcome, Pistol. I charge you with a drink.

Pistol: I stand to. I will discharge upon mine hostess.

Falstaff: She is Pistol proof.

Pistol: Then to you, Miss Doll! I will charge you.

Doll: Charge me! I scorn you, you base, rascally, cheating, lack linen fellow. I am an heiress. I am meat for your master.

Pistol: I know you, Miss Doll. Just because you wheedled two or three soldiers to leave you money in their will, is no reason to put on such airs. Miss Tearsheet, Miss Tearsheet!

Doll: Away you filth—you cutpurse, you pimp. To your bottle, or I'll thrust my knife in your chops.

Pistol: (menacing gesture) God let me die if I don't murder your clothes for this.

Quickly: No, good Captain, not here, sweet Captain.

Doll: Captain. You, a Captain!

Bardolph: Go down, Pistol.

Pistol: Not I. I tell you what, Corporal Bardolph. I could find it in my heart to bite her. I'll be revenged.

Falstaff: Better go down.

Pistol: I'll see her damned first.

Quickly: Good Captain Pistol—it is very late—aggravate your rage, I beseech you.

Pistol: What, shall pack horses compare with Caesar's and Hannibal's? Nay, damn them, let the welkin roar. Shall we fall foul for a whore?

Quickly: Faith, Captain, these are very bitter words—

Falstaff: Our Doll is grown into a lady.

Bardolph: This will grow into a brawl.

Pistol: Give me drink. (places his sword on the table) Sweetheart, lie thou there. Come we to swords' points here? And are *et ceteras* nothing?

Falstaff: Pistol, I would be alone.

Pistol: Then go to bed.

Doll: For God's sake thrust him downstairs— I cannot endure such a ranting rascal. He's fit company only for whores, not gentlewomen.

Pistol: As if a harlot could hide in a new smock. Thrust me downstairs!

Bardolph: Come, get you downstairs.

Pistol: What! Shall we have incision? Shall we imbrue? (snatches his sword) Then death rock me asleep, abridge my doleful days. Why, then let grievous, ghastly wounds, entwist the sisters three—come Atropos.

Falstaff: Hand me my rapier, Bardolph.

Doll: Dear Jack, do not draw.

Falstaff: Get you downstairs.

Quickly: Here's a goodly tumult. I'll foreswear keeping house afore I'll be in these fights.

(Falstaff thrusts at Pistol)

So! Murder. Put up your naked weapons.

(Falstaff drives Pistol out)

(Bardolph follows them out)

Doll: Jack, pray be easy. The rascal's gone. Ah, you whoreson, little valiant villain, you.

Quickly: Are you not hurt in the groin? He made a shrewd thrust at your body.

(Reenter Bardolph)

Falstaff, by William Shakespeare *et al.*

Falstaff: Have you turned him out?

Bardolph: Yes, the rascal's drunk. You have hurt him in the shoulder.

Falstaff: A rascal, to brave me!

Doll: Oh, you sweet little rogue! Faugh! How you sweat. Come let me wipe your face. Oh, rogue! I love thee. Thou are as valiant as Hector of Troy!

Falstaff: (aside) It takes.

(Aloud) A rascally slave. I will toss the rogue in a blanket.

Doll: Do!— And I'll keep you warm under a blanket.

Falstaff: Sit on my knee Doll. A rascal—braggart slave. The rogue fled from me like a frightened hare.

Doll: And you pursued him like an enraged elephant. When will you leave fighting a days and whoring a nights, and begin to patch up thy body for heaven?

(Enter Hal and Poins disguised not too well as waiters. They keep behind the other actors and turn away to avoid discovery during the following scene.)

Falstaff: Peace, Doll—do not speak like a death's head. Do not put me in mind of my end.

Doll: Tell me of the Prince then.

Falstaff: A promising youth. But he lacks style. I hate boasting, it is, however, well known what pains I have taken to make a man of that Hal. Before the greenhorn knew me he could not drink ale; made conscience of going to Church on holiday—and blushed like a scarlet cloak at talking price with a whore. I instructed him in all the manly exercises. I was content to win his money to teach him gaming; to get drunk myself that he might learn to hold his liquor. Setting rotten limbs and dignity aside, have I not even pimped for the bashful rogue? Such a Prince of Wales—I was ashamed of him. (Hal grimaces) Had it not been for me, he would be known as the Virgin King, and that's a shame even for a Queen.

Bardolph: It would have been a pity, Sir John.

Falstaff: A disgrace to England! Why, the Frenchies would never cease to laugh at us. Imagine an island so full of lusty whores and whore-masters with a sovereign still in knickers.

Bardolph: A national shame has been averted.

Falstaff: And then I taught him statecraft. It was I first taught him to take a purse: for I knew him when he durst not cry, "Stand!" to a turkey cock; is this fit for a statesman? A gander of the ordinary size of a green goose would have made him run for it. I went further yet, and taught him the manly art of conversation—in the style military, for instance or swearing.

Bardolph: Sir John, there, I believe, you forget yourself; the Prince wanted no assistance of you in that—for when he was a little crack, he would swear like a man six feet high.

Falstaff: Right, right. Swearing indeed he knew; for

though but a King's son, he would rap out an oath like an Emperor. But for the quintessence of elocution, the hyperbole—vulgarly called lying—there I am master. Yet what a deal of pains it has cost me to teach Hal to lie—imagine a statesman who cannot lie with a straight face. He would never do it roundly. He has no genius that way.

Hal: (aside) I shall learn, I shall learn.

Bardolph: He never had a way with it.

Doll: It's a pity all your efforts were thrown away upon him.

Falstaff: A very necessary part of his education. How will he ever shine in reciting his own exploits? Let Hal win a hundred battles, he will never be a Caesar, or a Falstaff.

Doll: I do not think you deserve to be made a lord, indeed.

Falstaff: 'Twere only fitting. For my well known economy I should be made Lord of the Exchequer. But it is not a just universe. Think of Belisarius and Alcibiades.

Bardolph: That was in King John's time, I think.

Falstaff: They were the Falstaffs of antiquity.

Doll: They say Poins has a good wit.

Falstaff: He a good wit? No more than a mallard duck. He can quack. He plays tennis well—and swears with a good grace; wears his stockings very smooth, and has all the other signs of a weak mind in an able body— for which the Prince adores him—for the Prince himself is just such another.

Hal: (to Poins) Would not this rascal have his ears cut off?

Poins: Let's beat him before his whore.

Hal: Is it not strange that desire should so many years outlive performance?

Falstaff: Kiss me, Doll.

Doll: (kissing him) I kiss you as I love you.

Falstaff: Thou dost give flattering busses. But I am old, I am old.

Doll: I love thee better than any a young scurvy boy of 'em all.

Falstaff: I shall receive money on Thursday. Will you have a new gown? Come, it grows late. We'll to bed. You'll forget me when I am gone.

Doll: (maudlin) You'll make me cry if you talk this way.

Falstaff: Some wine, boy.

Hal, Poins: Coming, sir, coming.

Falstaff: Ha! A bastard son of the King's—and are not you Poins, his brother?

Hal: Why you globe of sinfulness—what a life do you lead!

Falstaff: A better than yours, Sir. I am a gentleman, and you appear to be a servant, a drawer.

Hal: Very true, sir—and come to draw you out by the ears.

Quickly: Heaven preserve your Grace, welcome to London.

Falstaff: (leaning on and fondling Doll) Thou whoreson compound of mad majesty—by this flesh and corrupt blood, thou are welcome.

Doll: (primly) You fat fool—I scorn you.

Poins: He'll laugh you out of your just revenge and turn all to merriment if you take not heed.

Hal: You whoreson grease bag, you. How vilely did you speak of me even now before these honest, virtuous gentlewomen.

Doll: Now bless your royal heart, I am so.

Quickly: I thank, Your Majesty.

Falstaff: Did you hear me, Hal?

Hal: Yes, and you knew me, just as you knew me at Gadshill, and spoke to purpose to try my patience.

Falstaff: No, no. I did not think you were in hearing.

Hal: So you confess the abuse?

Falstaff: No abuse, Hal, on my honor, sweet Prince, no abuse.

Hal: Call me a virgin, and lacking in style, and I know not what.

Falstaff: No abuse, Hal.

Hal: This is not abuse. You admit the words, but deny the abuse.

Falstaff: None in the world. I dispraised you before the wicked that the wicked might not fall in love with you and lead you into corruption.

Doll: What do you say!

Quickly: I am no wicked!

Falstaff: In doing which, I have done the work of a careful friend, and a true subject; and your father is to give me thanks for it. No abuse, Hal; none, Ned, none; no boys, none.

Hal: Do you wrong these virtuous gentlewomen—and honest Bardolph whose zeal burns in his nose?

Poins: Answer that old stump, answer.

Falstaff: The fiend has marked down Bardolph irrevocably—his face is Hell's kitchen where sinners are toasted live over coals.

Hal: Now for these fine ladies—

Falstaff: For one of 'em, she is in Hell already, and burns poor souls, and for the other I owe her money and whether she be damned for that I know not.

Falstaff, by William Shakespeare *et al.*

(The ladies show great indignation)

Quickly: Who's that knocks so loud?

(Enter Nym)

Hal: What news, Nym?

Nym: My lord, the King your father is at Westminster. The Scots has risen.

Hal: Another rebellion? I am much to blame to spend my time so idly when I should be at my father's side. Give me my coat and sword. Jack, good night.

(Exit Hal and Poins)

Nym: I overtook a dozen of the watch asking for Sir John.

Falstaff: So we must go to the wars, again. This time I think I'll not go, unless I find a way to be shot-free.

Nym: Maybe that could be arranged. I've heard of a magician who for ten pounds will make a man safe from wound by gun or sword.

Falstaff: Do you say so? Ten pounds is a lot—but to be shot-free—

Nym: It's worth more than that.

Falstaff: Where is this fellow, what's his name?

Nym: He's an Irishman or a Welshman with some unpronounceable name.

Falstaff: Well, I'll see him. Now comes the sweet morsel of the night and we must hence and leave it unpicked.

(More knocking at the door)

What's the matter?

(Bardolph exits and returns)

Bardolph: You must away to court, sir, presently. A dozen Captains stay at the door for you. You have been promoted.

Falstaff: Pay the score, Bardolph. Farewell, hostess, farewell, Doll. You see, wenches, how men of merit are sought after. The Prince goes by himself, but the man of action is called for. Farewell, good wenches—

(Exit Falstaff magnificently)

(Bardolph follows)

Doll: I cannot speak—my heart is ready to burst. Well, sweet Jack, have a care of thy life.

Falstaff: (at the door) Farewell, farewell.

Quickly: Well, fare thee well. I have known thee these twenty years come Easter, but an honester, true hearted man—well fare thee well.

(The ladies sob)

Bardolph: (returning) Mrs. Tearsheet.

Quickly: What's the matter?

Bardolph: Bid Mrs. Tearsheet come to my master.

Quickly: Run. Doll, run, run good Doll!

BLACKOUT

SCENE 3

The Tavern, next day. Falstaff is taking his breakfast. He is a sloppy eater with pretensions of great gentility. Enter Doll.

Falstaff: Well my dear, Doll? What news poor jade, what news?

Doll: News! News that will make your old sinful heart go pit-a-pat. Blessed news!

Falstaff: Is the army discharged, the rebellion quashed?

Doll: No, no. I know nothing of that.

Falstaff: Disclose, Doll, disclose.

Doll: I come from Mrs. Ford.

Falstaff: Aha, you carried out your commission?

Doll: Yes, I can't think how to repay you for employing me in this way. Hark in your ear—

Falstaff: It needs not, Doll—it needs not. There is nobody near.

Doll: No matter for that. Secrets of this nature must be whispered.

Falstaff: (whispering) Come, come, Mrs. Ford—

Doll: She is the best natured creature breathing. Ah, you little wag, you little wanton puppy. (pointing to him) There's the face and the shape that have done it.

Falstaff: But what says she? What says she—be brief.

Doll: Why, she has received your letter.

(Aside) And compared it with mine.

Falstaff: Humph,—well?

Doll: And she says that her husband—

Falstaff: Well, what of him?

Doll: That he's a scurvy, filthy fellow and she can't abide him—so peevish, so jealous—

Falstaff: A plague on him. But to purpose, Doll, to purpose.

Doll: Why she says her husband will be out between three and four.

Falstaff: And I shall be in?

Doll: Between three and four. She says she will meet you.

(Aside) And will fit you.

(Aloud) She likes you better than any man in England, saving the Prince.

Falstaff: But where, Doll?

Doll: In her bed? Ah, you young, cursed rampant stallion, we must have you tied up

(Aside) and tied off—

(Aloud) in faith we must, Jack, if you run at your neighbor's mutton thus.

Falstaff: (panting) Where, where?

Doll: Why, in her house, of course. I'm going to her now. We must prepare everything so you are properly received.

(Exit Doll)

Falstaff: Dear, dear kindhearted, Doll. The best little whore in England.

(Falstaff resumes eating with increased appetite)

(Enter Bardolph)

Bardolph: Sir John, there's one master Brook below to speak with you. He has sent your worship a morning's draught.

(Presents a glass of wine)

Falstaff: Brook is his name?

Falstaff, by William Shakespeare *et al.*

Bardolph: Ay, sir.

Falstaff: Call him in. Brooks that overflow with wine are always welcome.

(Bardolph steps to the door, calls "Brook" and exits)

(Enter Hal, well disguised as a merchant)

Brook: Bless you, sir.

Falstaff: Would you speak with me? You're welcome, what's your name?

Brook: My name is Brook.

Falstaff: Good Master Brook, I desire more acquaintance of you.

Brook: I sue for yours, sir. I am emboldened. They say if money go before— all ways lie open.

Falstaff: Money's a good soldier.

Brook: Faith, I have a bag of money here troubles me. If you would help me to bear it—

Falstaff: (cunningly) I protest this must not be. I am not a Porter.

Brook: Twenty pounds, Sir John, is but a trifle—and I am not of the humor to trouble my friends for nothing, sir.

Falstaff: By no means, sir!

Brook: Good Sir John.

Falstaff, by William Shakespeare *et al.*

Falstaff: Nay, as I am a gentleman, as I am a gentleman, I am not a mercenary. (slight change of tone) How much is the sum, say you?

Brook: Twenty pounds, come you shall take it indeed, Sir John.

Falstaff: Sir, you are a perfect stranger to me.

Brook: Nay, it is in vain to struggle.

Falstaff: Sir, I shall not take it.

Brook: You must.

Falstaff: Upon my knighthood, I cannot.

Brook: Why there's ten more, Sir John.

Falstaff: Well, I am weak, I'm weak. I'm overpowered but in truth, I have reason to be abashed at this. Is it sterling? (biting it)

Brook: All good, upon my word, Sir John. And once more, I am sorry to be a perfect stranger to you.

Falstaff: No apologies, Master Brook. I am glad of your acquaintance and will serve you any way I can.

Brook: You are infinitely obliging, Sir John.

Falstaff: I am told you are an honest man, Master Brook.

(Aside) and downright fool, Master Brook.

Falstaff, by William Shakespeare *et al.*

Brook: I hope my inside will never give my outside the lie.

Falstaff: Your mind and your face speak the same language, Master Brook.

Brook: Too much compliments.

Falstaff: Could you but look into my mind, you would find me no complimentor— you would find that I esteem you as you justly deserve—something that would surprise you. But explain the business.

Brook: I am in love to an extremity.

Falstaff: (uneasily) Not with me, I hope?

Brook: No, no. With Mistress Margaret Ford. Beautiful Meg.

Falstaff: And have you loved her long?

Brook: These ten months.

Falstaff: And have you received satisfaction from her?

Brook: None.

Falstaff: And you have followed her like a sniveling dog?

Brook: Like a sniveling dog.

Falstaff: But when you have come up with her, she has kept you off with "Oh, my virtue, Oh, my honor, Oh, my sacred marriage vows," and the like drivel.

Falstaff, by William Shakespeare *et al.*

Brook: Her very words.

Falstaff: But, ah—you, ah—have conceived a shrewd suspicion that while she has been keeping you at bay some other dog is busy with her haunches?

Brook: You take it exactly.

Falstaff: Why, there it is, ha, ha, ha.

Brook: (angry) You are merry, Sir John.

Falstaff: She serves you for all the world as she does that cuckoldy rogue her husband.

Brook: (aside) Curse on him—does he know me?

Falstaff: With that sniveling gull, the slut passes for a saint.

Brook: Blood and Fire!

Falstaff: What say you, Master Brook?

Brook: I say you speak my heart's desire. Could I but detect her plainly— could I but prove she has been false to Ford—why then she could not— I should perfectly gain my point.

Falstaff: But, how Master Brook? For that particular I have forgot.

Brook: Why, she can pretend to virtue and honor no longer.

Falstaff: And you have the notion I can be serviceable to you in this.

Brook: I know, Sir John, you are a man of rare parts.

Falstaff: Sir.

Brook: Of singular learning.

Falstaff: Oh, sir.

Brook: Of incomparable address.

Falstaff: Good Master Brook.

Brook: You know the weakness of woman. Know how to leer, how to corrupt with a jest—

Falstaff: I have seduced many a virtuous maid, Master Brook.

Brook: Now, if you would but—

Falstaff: What, Master Brook?

Brook: Why, as it were—

Falstaff: Come, I'll help you out. Pimp for you, you would say.

Brook: Pimp is such a disagreeable word.

Falstaff: Come, we are men. No ceremony among friends. I'll do it, I'll do it. If I do not, may I be circumcised. You shall lie with Mrs. Ford this very night.

Brook: So soon!

Falstaff, by William Shakespeare *et al.*

Falstaff: Master Brook, I will first make bold with your money—next with your hand (shakes it) and last with your wench.

Brook: Oh, good sir.

Falstaff: As I am a gentleman, you shall sleep with her, enjoy her, man. As soon as I part with her myself.

Brook: You speak wonders—

Falstaff: I say you shall—

Brook: Want no money, Sir John. You shall want none.

Falstaff: Want no Mistress Ford—you shall want none. I shall be with her this day, this very afternoon—by her own appointment. Even as you came to me, her go between made me an appointment— Did you not see her leave?

Brook: (aside) Hell and Furies! Oh, the confounded Harlot!!!

Falstaff: What say you to it, Master Brook?

Brook: I say you could not do me a better service. Ford is already a—

Falstaff: A cuckold, Master Brook.

Brook: (aside) Oh, Devil!

(Aloud) But without jesting, Sir John.

Falstaff, by William Shakespeare *et al.*

Falstaff: An errant, downright, stinking cuckold.

(Brook whistles and walks around)

Falstaff: Do I speak well, Master Brook?

Brook: Like an angel

(Aside) with a cloven hoof.

(Aloud) You are positive?

(Falstaff smiles)

Dear, Sir John

(Aside) Damned, Sir John.

Falstaff: Am I a gentleman? Am I a knight? Would I lie to my bosom friend?

Brook: This is beyond my expectation. Are you sure of it?

Falstaff: Are you sure your name is Brook?

Brook: (starting) Of course.

Falstaff: (putting his fingers on Brook's head) He has done it here with a vengeance. Your business is done.

Brook: I am obliged to you, Sir John—and I shall endeavor to repay the obligation.

(Aside) I think I could murder this fat scoundrel.

Falstaff: Tonight, sweet wag, tonight.

Brook: Why do you call me wag?

Falstaff: Oh, it's an expression I use with my dearest friends. Tonight, you shall have blessed opportunity. I shall tell her that I will return about midnight. Then, then, opportunity man—strike while it's hot, I say.

Brook: (aside) Strike you through the guts.

Falstaff: Ford has the most forfeited forehead and the weakest pericranium of any cuckold in Christendom. The rogue shall butt with any bull of Basham.

Brook: My head, my head.

Falstaff: What's the matter, Brook?

Brook: You have roused me from the dead.

Falstaff: Tonight there shall be resurrection, Master Brook—resurrection!

Brook: Where do you meet her?

Falstaff: At her brother's house.

Brook: (aside) Does he pimp for his sister? What a devil of a tribe am I fallen into?

Falstaff: You look pale, Master Brook.

Brook: With too much expectation.

Falstaff: Has my discourse warmed you?

Falstaff, by William Shakespeare *et al*.

Brook: I am on fire. You have raised a transport in me.

Falstaff: Ha, ha, lechery! Ah, I was a young lecher once. Those were the days. Now, I am merely an old sinner. But in a few hours hence you will find me doing execution between a pair of sheets.

Brook: With Meg?

Falstaff: Not actually with her. But waiting as she is stripping herself for the encounter. Does the fancy take you, Master Brook.

Brook: To distraction.

Falstaff: Her gown just slipping off—

Brook: Sir John.

Falstaff: Her underpetticoat falling about her heels.

Brook: Good Sir John.

Falstaff: And then her lily white arm stretched out and her milk white bubbees displayed.

(Pause, Brook writhes)

The bed clothes just turning up.

Brook: Oh.

Falstaff: And one of her buxom naked legs raised to enter the bed—

Brook: Devil, devil, devil—

Falstaff: (laughing) Well, I will have mercy. Learn to woo from me, young man.

(Exit Falstaff)

Brook: Damned, epicurean rascal. See the Hell of having a false woman. And I cannot even protect myself because she is another man's wife. Damn her. Damn him, damn her— Damn them both!

BLACKOUT

Scene 4

A room in Mrs. Ford's house. Enter Doll Tearsheet dressed like a man with a patch over her eye.

Doll: Meg.

Mrs. Ford: Doll. Well, you look for all the world like a swaggering little whoremaster.

Doll: From whore to whoremaster, I like it. You look very languishing today.

Mrs. Ford: These languishing eyes have done a devilish deal of mischief lately, they have mauled a giant.

Doll: Sure he thinks our needs must be very pressing to dare to make love to us both, and then to ask me to carry a message to you.

Mrs. Ford: I had rather lie under a whale than lie with him. What tempest threw him ashore with so many tuns of oil in his belly at my door?

Doll: Have you prepared everything according to our plan?

Mrs. Ford: I have. He'll be lucky to escape this house alive.

Doll: Then I shall retire and appear as agreed.

Mrs. Ford: Content.

(Exit Doll. Mrs. Ford after a moment checks the room, inspects a hamper of clothes, then goes out. Enter Falstaff.)

Falstaff: Well, old Jack, go thy ways. I'll make more of thy old body than I have done. Will a woman yet look after thee? Wilt thou, after so much expense of money be now a gainer? Good body, I thank thee. Let them say 'tis grossly done, so it be fairly done—no matter. (the clock strikes) Soft—the bell struck three. The minute draws on. Now, the hot-blooded gods assist me. Remember, Jove, thou wast a bull for thy Europa—love set on thy horns. Oh powerful love that makes a beast a man and a man a beast. You were also, Jove, a swan for love of Leda. Oh omnipotent love, how near the God drew to the complexion of a goose! A fault done first in the form of a beast. Oh, Jove, a beastly fault. When gods have hot backs, what shall poor men do? Send me a cool rut time, Jove, or who can blame me to press my tallow! Who comes here?

(Enter Mrs. Ford)

Mrs. Ford: Sir John, are you here my dear?

Falstaff: Have I caught thee, heavenly jewel? Why now,

let me die, for I have lived long enough: this is the period of my ambition. Oh, this blessed hour.

Mrs. Ford: Oh, sweet Sir John.

Falstaff: Sweet Meg, I cannot, Meg, I cannot prate. Now shall I sin in my thoughts, I would your husband were dead. I would make thee my lady.

Mrs. Ford: Truly, I have wished him dead that I might be free for some time. But I would make a pitiful lady.

Falstaff: Let the court of France show me such another. You should be Queen.

Mrs. Ford: Do you think so? I like that idea.

Falstaff: A French bonnet would become you mightily.

Mrs. Ford: A plain kerchief, Sir John.

Falstaff: You are a tyrant to say so. You would make an absolute courtier. I see what you would be if fortune were your friend. Come, you cannot hide it.

Mrs. Ford: Believe me, there's no such thing in me.

Falstaff: What made me love you? Let that persuade you there's something extraordinary in you. I love you—none but you—and you deserve it.

Mrs. Ford: I heard you love Mistress Doll Tearsheet.

Falstaff: You might as well suggest I love to walk by an open sewer.

(Doll puts her head around the corner when this is said)

Mrs. Ford: Heaven knows how I love you,—and you shall soon find it.

Falstaff: I'll deserve it.

Mrs. Ford: You say you love me?

Falstaff: Do I love sherry? Do I love sack and sugar? You are sweeter to me than either of them.

(There is a loud knocking)

Falstaff: Who's that?

(Mrs. Ford looks and returns upset)

Mrs. Ford: This is the most detracting and insolent fellow. If he should but find you in the room he'd swear he saw you in bed with me.

Falstaff: Shall I terrify him a little with my cudgel?

Mrs. Ford: No, no. Better hide behind the curtains. He will persuade a woman who tells him she scorns him that she lay with him the night before.

(Falstaff hides behind the drapes)

(Enter Doll dressed as Captain Snipe)

Falstaff: (peeping) What abridgement of man is this?

Mrs. Ford: What business brings you hither, Captain Snipe?

Snipe: Can't you guess?

Mrs. Ford: No.

Snipe: Why, the same that I had when I was here last with you.

Mrs. Ford: When was that, pray?

Snipe: Have you forgot? Come, come, to bed. I'll refresh your memory. Are you alone?

Mrs. Ford: No, I have a very troublesome, impudent fellow with me.

Snipe: Ha— Demme, I shall beat your cuckold for that affront.

Falstaff: What measuring stick is this?

Snipe: Don't oblige me to force nature—by this kiss (kissing her) I am inclined to be the best natured creature in the world.

Mrs. Ford: Nay, Captain.

Snipe: And this.

Mrs. Ford: Fie, Captain.

Snipe: And this.

Mrs. Ford: Nay, dear Captain.

Falstaff: If I remain concealed a little longer, Ford and I are like to be brothers in a way I did not dream of.

Mrs. Ford: Know vile man that I have a protector in Sir John Falstaff who will not permit you to treat me thus.

Snipe: Sir John Falstaff. Ha, ha, ha. I am now come from the Prince and Poins with whom I have had such a banquet of laughter at that fat fool.

Mrs. Ford: At him?

Snipe: Oh, he's a perpetual jest, an everlasting comedy. Why, yesterday there was a bastard laid to him by the parish fool. And this morning he entered a course of physick to cure the French disease.

Falstaff: (coming forward) Villain, thou liest.

Snipe: Have mercy on me.

Falstaff: Mary and amen, for you have not three minutes to live.

Snipe: What have we here, a ghost, a fat ghost?

Falstaff: I'll make you feel I am no ghost.

Snipe: Demme, I'll make you one.

Mrs. Ford: Good Captain, Good Sir John.

Falstaff: Stand off woman. Do you think I'll be overcome by this sign post—this picture of a man?

Snipe: Why, thou rumbling dung cart—

Falstaff, by William Shakespeare *et al.*

Falstaff: Why, thou weasel, thou rabbit a tiptoe, thou Jack a lanthorn.

Snipe: Peace you fat fool.

Falstaff: Why thou whimsy, thou illusion. Oh, for more breath, oh, for some wind of utterances.

(Enter Male Servant of Snipe's)

Servant: Sir, a word with you.

Snipe: What is it?

Servant: Begone if you love yourself, and flee.

Snipe: Why?

Servant: The officer that you pistolled last night in Cheapside is dead of his wounds.

Snipe: How, dead?

Servant: The watch is looking for you.

Falstaff: Who would have thought this pigmy was such a kill cow?

Mrs. Ford: Would to heaven we were both out of his hands.

Falstaff: Would I were dead drunk at the Boar's Head.

Mrs. Ford: (to Snipe) 'Twere better you leave.

Snipe: We know your meaning. Leave so that you may

gratify your base desires. I'll kill him.

Mrs. Ford: Why, can you think I am in love with this knight? Is this a creature for a woman to love? He has been a by word among all women that ever knew him.

Falstaff: The truth's the truth, and who will say Jack Falstaff ever told a lie or scorned to admit the truth.

Mrs. Ford: What, jealous of me with a porpoise, Captain? If my desires were so preposterous, how could I bring it about?

Falstaff: Consider that, Captain, consider that.

Mrs. Ford: I assure you he has it not in his power.

Falstaff: You have hit it. You have hit it.

Mrs. Ford: I don't believe he knows what a woman is—

Falstaff: If I do, I am a villain. If I have not forgot whether lust be a pleasure or a pain, I am no two legged creature. About two years ago I got in bed with a cheesemonger's wife, and if I was not carted out of bed by her and kicked like a football, may I be circumcised like an 'Ebrew.

Snipe: Well, Sir John, you say you had no design upon Mrs. Ford.

Falstaff: Upon my knighthood, none in the least.

Snipe: To show how heartily I am reconciled to you, give me your hand old boy. Will you do me the office of a friend?

Falstaff: Why what would a man not do to oblige a friend?

Snipe: Good, good. For reasons I have hinted to you, I would gladly take my leave of this gentlewoman in private and without interruption. Now for friendship's sake do you stand at the door while she and I go to the next room—and say our goodbyes. You shall be our noble sentry.

Falstaff: You make a modest and reasonable request. But being pimp in ordinary to the royal family, do you see, Prince Hall has sworn me to confine my talent that way.

Snipe: Sir, if you do not I will shoot you through the head.

Falstaff: Mrs. Ford?

Mrs. Ford: My dear.

Falstaff: What do you resolve to do?

Mrs. Ford: To save you, Sir John, whatever come of it.

Falstaff: Who says this is not a loving, tender-hearted, charitable creature?

Mrs. Ford: Do you think I can stand to see you shot through the head?

Falstaff: (aside) Rather than that she'll choose to be run through the body herself.

Mrs. Ford: 'Tis but humoring him, you know, for the moment.

Falstaff: That's it. Humoring him.

Mrs. Ford: Dear Sir John, you see what I do to protect you.

Falstaff: I do indeed, I see it plainly.

(Mrs. Ford and Snipe go out, Falstaff paces up and down; the Servant returns.)

Servant: Mr. Snipe, you must escape, the watch know you are here.

(Reenter Snipe and Mrs. Ford, Snipe buttoning his trousers)

Snipe: Was ever man so unkindly interrupted. Goodbye, M'dear. Adieu, Sir John.

(Exit Snipe with Servant)

Mrs. Ford: At last he is gone.

Falstaff: Did the little cur harm you, if he did—?

Mrs. Ford: He did me no hurt, no injury—

Falstaff: I am glad or I should have killed him. He was civil?

Mrs. Ford: Very civil. He shewed himself a gentleman in all his parts.

Falstaff: So. But now my dear, time runs for us—

Falstaff, by William Shakespeare *et al*.

Mrs. Ford: (embracing him) Sir John, dear, Sir John.

Falstaff: This may turn out well, after all.

(Enter another Servant)

Servant: Mrs. Ford, Mrs. Ford, here's Mrs. Page at the door, sweating and blowing, and needs will speak with you presently.

Falstaff: She shall not see me. I will ensconce behind the curtain.

Mrs. Ford: Pray you do so, she's a very tattling woman.

(Falstaff hides, enter Doll as Mrs. Page.)

Mrs. Page: Oh, Mrs. Ford, what have you done? You're shamed, you're overthrown, you're undone forever.

Mrs. Ford: What's the matter?

Mrs. Page: Your husband's coming hither with a crowd to search the premises for a man he says is in the house. You are undone.

Mrs. Ford: 'Tis not so, I hope.

Mrs. Page: (maliciously) Pray heaven you haven't got a man here. This time! But 'tis most certain your husband's coming with half the town at his heels. If you know yourself clear, I am glad for it. If you have a friend here, convey him, convey him out.

Mrs. Ford: What shall I do? There is a gentleman here.

Mrs. Page: Oh, my dear friend. And you denied it to my face. Well, I'll help you anyway, for the honor of our sex. If he be of any reasonable stature he may creep in here, throw foul linen on him as it were, and have it carried out.

Mrs. Ford: He's too big to get in there.

(Falstaff comes out of hiding)

Falstaff: Let me see, let me see. I can do it, I can do it. 'Tis only scrooching up my legs a little. I'll in, I'll in. (he awkwardly attempts to get in)

Mrs. Page: What, Sir Falstaff? Oh Mrs. Ford, Mrs. Ford, I never knew you liked such moldy meat. Well, cover him with dirty linen.

(They display some truly filthy linen.)

Mrs. Page: Call your men, call your men, and have them take these clothes to the laundress by the Thames, quickly.

(Two men enter, pick up the hamper and stagger out)

Mrs. Ford: Timothy, James. Deliver this to the laundress.

(Aside) And dump the contents into the muddiest part of the river.

(Exit servants with hamper)

Mrs. Page, Mrs. Ford: (both) Ha, ha, ha.

Mrs. Ford: Was it not brave?

Doll: I am revenged.

Mrs. Ford: And I.

Doll: Wait till the Prince learns of it.

Mrs. Ford: I'll see that he hears. I promise you.

Doll: Ha, ha, ha.

BLACKOUT

SCENE 5

Mrs. Ford's room, a little later. Hal is talking with Mrs. Ford.

Hal: Pish. Tell me no tales of a cock and a bull, Meg.

Mrs. Ford: You don't believe me, ask Doll Tearsheet.

Hal: Who would believe that whore? You do not choose reliable witnesses.

Mrs. Ford: Then ask Falstaff himself.

Hal: By now he has sworn he slept with you for a month. And faith, he may not be lying.

Mrs. Ford: You use me well, Prince Harry, do you?

Hal: Ay, I do so.

Mrs. Ford: Heaven make you better than your thoughts.

Hal: Amen.

Mrs. Ford: You do yourself mighty wrong, Master Brook.

Hal: Ay, ay, I must bear it.

Mrs. Ford: The only thing worse than a jealous husband, is a jealous lover.

Hal: I suspect without cause, Mistress Meg?

Mrs. Ford: Heaven be my witness, you do, if you suspect me of any dishonesty to you, even with my husband.

Hal: Well said, brazen-face—hold it out.

Mrs. Ford: Are you not ashamed?

Hal: I shall find you yet.

(Exit Hal)

Mrs. Ford: A woman can be honest for all she is light hearted and gay. He's gone. Oh, Harry, you deserve to suffer the jealousy you feel.

BLACKOUT

Scene 6

The Inn, next morning. Falstaff eating his morning meal. Soldiers beat each other on, then off stage. Falstaff ignores them, occasionally throws a bone at them.

Falstaff: Let all the world be cheated, for I have been cheated and beaten, too. If it should come to the ear of the court how I have been transformed and how my transformation has been washed, they would melt me out of my fat, drop by drop. Ah, I never prospered since I foreswore myself at cards. Well, if my wind were but long enough, I might repent.

(Enter Doll Tearsheet)

Doll: Good morrow, Sir John, you puppy you.

Falstaff: (grumpily) Now whence come you?

Doll: From the party, from the party.

Falstaff: The devil take the party—I have suffered more for her sake—more than the villainous inconstancy of man's disposition is able to bear.

Doll: And has she not suffered? Mrs. Ford is beaten black and blue, that you cannot see a white spot on her.

Falstaff: What tell you me of black and blue? I was dumped in the mud by the Thames and almost taken for a witch but for my admirable dexterity of wit in counterfeiting an old woman with child that saved me, the constable had set me in the stocks, in the public stocks for a witch.

Doll: Mrs. Ford is determined to reward your sufferings for her to the very extremity of her ability. She bids you come again tonight. Her husband is a birding.

Falstaff: No more prattling; I will come. I owe it to myself.

Doll: Fare you well, you old tom cat.

FALSTAFF, BY WILLIAM SHAKESPEARE *ET AL.*

(Exit Doll)

Falstaff: I hope good luck lies in even numbers tonight. Bardolph, Bardolph, I say!

Bardolph: (entering) Here, sir.

Falstaff: Go fetch me a pot of ale.

(Exit Bardolph)

Have I lived to be carried in a basket, like a barrow of butcher's offal, and to be thrown into the Thames? Well, if I be served such another trick, I'll have my brains taken out and buttered and give them to a dog for a Christmas present. The rogues threw me in the river with as little remorse as they would have drowned a blind bitch's puppy. By my size I have a kind of alacrity in sinking. If the bottom was deep as Hell, I should drown. I had been drowned but that it was very shallow—and that death I abhor—for the water swells a man, and what a thing should I have been when I had been swelled! I should have been a mountain of mummy.

(Enter Bardolph with ale)

Falstaff: Come, let me pour some ale into the Thames water—my belly's as cold as if I had swallowed snowballs.

(Enter Brook, exit Bardolph)

Brook: Bless you, sir.

Falstaff: Now, Master Brook, you come to know what has

passed between me and Ford's wife.

Brook: That indeed, Sir John, is my business.

Falstaff: Master Brook, I will not lie to you: I was at her house at the hour appointed.

Brook: And sped you, sir?

Falstaff: Very ill, Master Brook.

Brook: (aside) Perhaps Meg's honest.

(Aloud) How so, Sir? Did she change her determination?

Falstaff: No, no, Master Brook. But there happened things between us that shame and modesty will not let me tell.

Brook: (aghast) We shall conceal nothing from our friends, Sir John.

Falstaff: You are in the right. Lord, lord, how the world is given to lying. Well, to be short, Master Brook, that sneaking husband of hers, dwelling in a continual alarum of jealousy, comes in the very crisis of our conversation.

Brook: How, the crisis?

Falstaff: Ay, the crisis. After we had embraced, kissed, protested, and as it were, finished the prologue to our comedy, in comes the husband, at his heels the entire rabble of Eastcheap, to search his house.

Brook: What, while you were there?

Falstaff, by William Shakespeare *et al.*

Falstaff: While I was there. And were I not still nimble he had caught us almost in flagrante.

Brook: And did he find you?

Falstaff: You shall hear. As good luck would have it, in comes Mistress Page, a neighbor, to warn Mrs. Ford of her cuckoldy husband's approach.

Brook: Sure, that was a lucky chance.

Falstaff: Very lucky. She had the invention to convey me hence in a clothes hamper.

Brook: This is extraordinary. A clothes hamper?

Falstaff: Aye, a clothes hamper. Rammed me in with foul shirts and smocks—old stockings, greasy napkins, beshitted underwear—the rankest compound of villainous smell, Master Brook, that ever offended human nostril.

Brook: And how long lay you there?

Falstaff: You shall hear what I have suffered to bring this woman to evil for your good. Being thus crammed in the basket two servants carried me in the name of foul clothes to Datchet Lane, and met their master in the street. I quaked for fear lest the lunatic knave would have searched the basket, but fate ordaining that he should be a cuckold held his hand. On he went to search and away I went for foul clothes. But mark the sequel. A man of my kidney, as subject to heat as butter; a man of continual dissolution and thaw—it was a miracle to escape suffocation. And in the height of this dirty bath, when I was more than half stewed—in grease—like a

Dutch cheese—to be thrown into the Thames and cooled, glowing hot in that surge, like a horseshoe, think of that—hissing hot—think of that, Master Brook.

Brook: (smiling) Then you will undertake no more?

Falstaff: I will be thrown into Vesuvius, into Etna, ere I will leave it thus. Her husband after beating his wife is gone a birding. I have received another embassy of meeting for this very night.

Brook: Have you so?

(Aside) Damned whore.

Falstaff: I must dress for my appointment. Come at your leisure, and you shall know all. In conclusion Master Brook, you shall cuckold Ford—you shall, you shall or I am not Jack Falstaff.

(Exit Falstaff)

Brook: Is this a vision? Is this a dream? Will Fat Jack cuckold the Prince of Wales? This it is to be in love. To keep a woman. Can a keeper, like a husband, have horns? Oh, Meg, you are false to your adulterous vows to me.

(Enter Poins)

Poins: I thought I'd find you here.

Brook: What's the matter?

Poins: You must come to court. It's thought your father is dying.

Falstaff, by William Shakespeare *et al.*

Brook: Great God, and I stand fooling thus. Away.

BLACKOUT

Scene 7

A royal apartment. The King asleep on a couch. The King resembles Falstaff in many ways, like Falstaff he is both fat and old, but where Falstaff is gay, merry, and open, the King is reserved, grave, and crafty. The King wakes. [This scene may be omitted in presentation.]

King: Warwick! Gloucester, Clarence!

(Enter Prince John)

Prince John: What would, Your Majesty?

King: Why did you leave me here alone?

Prince John: We left Prince Harry here—who undertook to sit and watch by you.

King: The Prince of Wales? Where is he? Let me see him.

Prince John: He is not here. This door is open—he is gone away.

King: Where is the crown? Who took it from my pillow?

Prince John: It was by your pillow.

King: The Prince has taken it hence. Go find him.

(Exit Prince John)

Oh, Harry, are you in such haste to be King? It will be soon enough. This helps end me. See, see what sons are—

(Enter Hal with the crown)

Hal: I never thought to hear you speak again, father.

King: The wish was father to that thought. I stay too long for you. Do you hunger so for my death?

Hal: You misunderstand me, father.

BLACKOUT

CURTAIN

ACT FOUR

SCENE 1

A street near the palace. Enter Prince John meeting the Chief Justice with his Aide.

Prince John: Whither away, my Lord Chief Justice?

Chief Justice: How does the King?

Prince John: Exceeding well, his cases now are all ended.

Chief Justice: I would His Majesty had called me with him. The services I performed for him have made me many enemies.

Prince John: Indeed, I think my brother loves you not.

Chief Justice: I know he does not.

(Enter Hal as King)

Chief Justice: (bowing) God save Your Majesty.

Hal: God save you from my Majesty. You look strangely on me. You are, I think, fearful I love you not.

Falstaff, by William Shakespeare *et al.*

Chief Justice: If you measure justly, Your Majesty has no cause to hate me.

Hal: No? Why do I then? How might a prince of my great hopes so forget the indignities you had put upon me? What! Berate and roughly send me to prison—the immediate heir of England? Was this easy?

Chief Justice: I then represented your father. The dignity of his power lay then in me. Your Highness was pleased to forget my place and struck me while I occupied the bench—the very seat of justice. If you judge the deed ill—

Hal: I do—

Chief Justice: Then be contented to have a son set your decrees at naught, and have no one to enforce your will.

Hal: You are right. But the injury I will not forgive. You need not fear reprisal but do not expect my favor.

Chief Justice: Let me earn my pardon.

Hal: You must do me great service to induce me to forget such insults.

Chief Justice: (presenting a scroll) I have bethought me of one. This document does prove thee to be the lawful heir to the throne of France.

Hal: (surprised and interested) Well, well, I'll think on it.

(Exit Hal and Prince John)

Chief Justice: (to his Aide) Go take this purse of a thou-

Falstaff, by William Shakespeare *et al.*

sand pounds to Sir John Falstaff. Go this instant.

Aide: My Lord.

BLACKOUT

Scene 2

A Street. Falstaff and Bardolph meeting Pistol.

Falstaff: How now, Pistol?

Pistol: Sir John, God save you.

Falstaff: What wind blew you hither, Pistol?

Pistol: Not an ill one, sweet knight, you are now the second greatest man in the realm.

Falstaff: Second? I am the first. Do you wish to insult me?

Pistol: Sir John, I am thy Pistol and thy friend. And helter-skelter have I rode to thee and joyful tidings do I bring.

Falstaff: Deliver them like a man of this world.

Pistol: A fart for the world, and worldlings base. I speak of Africa and golden joys.

Falstaff: (shaking him) What is thy news?

Pistol: Sir John, thy tender lamb kin, thy adopted child— is King. Harry the Fifth's the man.

Falstaff: Is old Bolingbroke dead?

Falstaff, by William Shakespeare *et al.*

Pistol: As a nail in the door.

Falstaff: Away Bardolph, saddle my horse. Choose what office thou wilt and 'tis thine. Pistol, for this good news I will doubly charge you with dignities.

Bardolph: Oh, joyful days, I would not take a fortune for this luck—

Pistol: What, do I bring good news?

Falstaff: Bardolph—Lord Bardolph—be what you will. I am Fortune's steward. Get ready, we'll ride all night. Boot—boot. I know the young King is sick for me. Let us take any horses that we find, the laws of England are at my command. Blessed are they that have been my friends and woe to my Lord Chief Justice.

Pistol: Sir, it is unnecessary to ride to court for the King himself is coming even now.

Falstaff: See how he loves me; he couldn't wait. Stand by me Pistol, I will make the King do you grace. I will leer upon him as he comes by—and do but mark his looks.

Pistol: God bless your lungs, good knight.

(Enter the Chief Justice's Aide)

Aide: Sir John, Sir John.

Falstaff: What would you, still begging? Or soon will be.

Aide: No, Sir John, bearing gifts. The Lord Chief Justice has bethought him that you asked for a loan of a thousand pounds, and sends it to you that you may remember him as a friend.

Falstaff: Well, this is kind. (takes the purse) Tell him I will endeavor to do him justice.

Aide: I will, sweet knight.

(Exit Aide)

Pistol: God bless your lungs, good knight.

Falstaff: Come here, Bardolph, stand behind me. If I had time I would get new clothes—but it's no matter. It looks better as it is, as it shows the zeal with which we come to attend him.

Bardolph: It does so.

Falstaff: It shows my earnestness of affection.

Pistol: That's it, that's it.

Falstaff: My devotion.

Bardolph: It does, it does, it does.

Falstaff: As if there were nothing else to be done but to see him.

Bardolph: So indeed.

Pistol: My knight, I will inflame thy noble liver. Thy Doll—the Helen of thy noble thoughts is in base durance and contagious prison haled by the most dirty watch. Rouse up thy revenge. Doll is taken.

Falstaff, by William Shakespeare *et al.*

Falstaff: I will deliver her.

(Trumpets)

Pistol: There roared the sea—

(Enter Hal and the Lord Chief Justice, attended)

Falstaff: God save thy Grace, King Hal, my royal Hal.

Pistol: Heaven guard thee and keep thee.

Falstaff: God save thee, my sweet boy.

Hal: My Lord Chief Justice, speak to that vain man.

Chief Justice: Have you your wits? Know you what it is you speak?

Falstaff: My King, my Jove! I speak to thee my heart!

Hal: (to the astonishment of all, not the least the Lord Chief Justice) I know thee not, old man. Fall to thy prayers. How ill white hairs become a fool and a jester. So old—so profane— Reply not to me with a jest. Presume not that I am the thing that I was. Reform, Falstaff, reform. Take example from me.

(To the Lord Chief Justice) Let it be your care to see my will performed.

(Exit the King and all his party)

Falstaff: (recovering) I shall be sent for in private to him. He must seem thus to the world. Fear not the advancement—I will be the man yet, that will make you all great.

Bardolph: I cannot well perceive how, unless you should give me your clothes and stuff me up with straw. Fare you well, Sir John.

Pistol: Goodbye, Sir John.

Bardolph: Fare you well.

(Exit Pistol and Bardolph)

Falstaff: This is but a pretence—a pretence. I will be sent for. (shouting) I will be sent for.

(Falstaff is all alone; the street empty.)

CURTAIN

Scene 3

Later the same day, the Boarshead Tavern.

Quickly: Is Sir John coming?

Bardolph: He will be here incontinently, hostess.

Doll: Has Falstaff got money by him?

Bardolph: Yes,—a thousand pounds. The Chief Justice sent it to him before the coronation.

Quickly: What—I thought he was Sir John's enemy?

Bardolph: He was. But on the old King's death he was a

little afraid of Prince Hal, and thought to engratiate himself with the new King through Sir John. The Lord Chief Justice is a courtier.

Doll: I'll marry him, that's sure.

Quickly: Will you so, will you so. He's engaged to me.

Bardolph: Ladies, ladies. But Mrs. Doll, how came you from the watch?

Doll: I had to give money—that's all.

(Doll becomes suddenly subdued)

(Enter Sir John panting)

Doll: Oh, here's Sir John himself.

Quickly: Jaded to death, I warrant. An easy chair, good Bardolph. Please to depose yourself, Sir John.

(From this point on, Quickly and Doll engage in a sort of silent competition in doing things to please Falstaff)

Falstaff: So—a glass of sherry.

(Quickly darts for it)

Doll: (sashaying up to him) And how do you find yourself, my sweet knight?

Falstaff: Thirsty—I can drink—and that is all the bodily functions I am capable of—I am as stiff as a sign post—every part of me.

Falstaff, by William Shakespeare *et al*.

Doll: Nay, Sir John, if you be stiff—all is not over with you yet. Give me a buss.

Falstaff: Go, Doll, you are riggish—get you gone you wag tail, you. I am not merrily disposed.

Doll: Will you give me a new skirt?

Falstaff: I will Doll, I will. Nay, I cannot bear you on my knee.

Doll: Why, how came you so terribly mauled, my little porpoise?

Falstaff: Did I not tell you?

Quickly: (placing herself between Doll and Sir John) You did not descend to particles, Sir John.

Falstaff: Well then, I will tell you. You must know that the King—hang him for a sheep stealing cur—gave me the rebuff and stalked off like he did not know me, leaving me to the mercy of the multitude.

(Doll and Quickly voice astonishment)

Falstaff: Put not your faith in Princes. How true the saying is. Well, there I was jammed in the midst of a vile group of mechanics—as if we had grown together in a body corporate. By and by this fair belly was pressed as flat as a Christmas pancake. It is a miracle I did not burst in the midst of them.

Doll: If you had, Sir John, you would have gone off with a bang—like a burst bladder.

Falstaff, by William Shakespeare *et al.*

Falstaff: I should have died a hero. My exit would have made some noise in the world.

Quickly: Heaven forbid you should die a virulent death.

Doll: I hope indeed, sweet knight, you will never be pressed to death.

Quickly: You was more inhumanly used. Would nobody take pity on you?

Falstaff: Pity—your London rabble is the most remorseless rascal. They made no more of me than if I had been a lump of dough they were kneading into dumplings.

Doll: Why did you not exert your courage, Sir John, and draw upon them?

Falstaff: I could not come at my rapier to be master of a kingdom. And as for good words—in return for the few I gave them, they let their jests so thick upon me that I was dumbfounded.

Doll: I thought you could never have been over matched that way, Sir John.

Falstaff: Two to one, Doll. They pelted me from all quarters. Will you hear? A dried eel skin of a fishmonger asked me how a porpoise could be ill at ease amidst a glut of herrings and minnows. I had not time to answer the dirty smelt when a barber surgeon—the very model of a skeleton offered to tap me for the dropsy, and to make a little room by letting out a barrel of wine at my waist. "Right" cries a third, "it's a hogshead of Spanish wine disguised as a man. Tap him, tap him, Master surgeon." I was forced to draw in my horns lest the villains being thirsty should force the shaver to perform the operation. I might otherwise have been drunk up alive.

(Enter Nym)

Nym: Sir Knight, I bring you good news. Local fame reports my Lord Chief Justice has withdrawn his warrants, but we are to stay from the King at least ten miles on pain of imprisonment.

Falstaff: Would he were choked with his warrants. But I thank thee for the tidings. Set up drinks for all. I'll bet the Chief Justice would like his thousand pounds back. Well, he may whistle for it. Times are not so bad, hostess, but we may yet have a merry burst at Eastcheap. The gross indignity Hal has put upon me sticks in my throat—yet I will endeavor to wash it down. I will turn cobbler ere I have to do with blood royal again. Ingratitude! I hate it. Put not your faith in Princes!

Doll: But is it true you have a thousand pounds, Sir John?

Falstaff: It is with my banker even now.

Doll: Then you may ask me anything, Sir John—see if I refuse you.

Quickly: Impudent hussy!!

(Quickly and Doll go off to the side and squabble in dumb show)

Falstaff: How is it with Pistol, Bardolph?

Bardolph: Sir John, he is in a bad way, the crowd almost trampled him.

Falstaff, by William Shakespeare *et al.*

Falstaff: Who ever knew you or Pistol in a good way?

Bardolph: And yet, Sir John, we are your followers.

Falstaff: Well said, Bardolph. I see your wit is improving.

Bardolph: The doctor says he may die if he is not bled.

Falstaff: Bled, how much?

Bardolph: Sixteen ounces.

Falstaff: Has the doctor a design against his life? If Pistol be not hanged he shall die a natural death. Poor Pistol, I would not lose him—for though he be a worthless knave, he is an old friend; and I never could find it in my heart to part with old friends merely because they are good for nothing. King Hal is another sort of man. Poor Pistol.

Bardolph: It was lucky for us all that we got off as well as we did.

Falstaff: You left me in the lurch!

Bardolph: Pon honor, Sir John, I did my utmost to keep up with you but it was impossible. I was lucky I myself was not trod to death.

Falstaff: You! Why, have I not seen you clear the ring without a cudgel at a bear baiting? You might make your way through a legion, nay, the millions of a crusade. Who dares come within a fathom of that firebrand, thy nose? They fear it will burn their holiday clothes, you would have set them blazing like stubble, and consumed whole processions of heralds like men of straw. A plague upon them. It was by their avoiding of you, that I had like to have died a martyr to corpulency.

Bardolph: Sir John, you're always plaguing me about my face. What would you have me do with it?

Falstaff: Do with it? If there were water enough in the Thames, I'd have you quench it. God forgive me, but when you would run behind a hedge for fear of the watch, I could not help comparing you to Moses and the burning bush.

Bardolph: (angry) I would it were out, so I might hear no more on it. If I must always be your butt, Sir John, I will seek another service, I assure you.

Falstaff: No, no, good Bardolph, that must not be. I speak not in disparagement —heaven knows I mean to cherish thee against lack of fuel or the visitation of a Dutch winter.

Bardolph: 'Sblood, Sir John, I'll bear it no longer.

Falstaff: Stay, I shall need you to warm me under the coldness of the King's displeasure.

Bardolph: Hot wine would do you more good, for I am as cold as any fish, whatever light I may give.

Falstaff: Cold—your face would condemn you for an incendiary before any bench of the judicature in the kingdom! You carry apparent combustibles into court with you. Certain—you would have been hanged long ago had not the sheriff been afraid you would have scorched the hangman or the gibbet.

Falstaff, by William Shakespeare *et al.*

Bardolph: Well, Sir John, I have been your attendant these twenty years—and I don't find I have had any such effect on you.

Falstaff: The cause, you rogue, the cause! Am I not obliged to keep ale and wine constantly discharging on me to keep me from blazing? Mark me walking but a hundred paces with thee glowing at my heels, if I do not broil and drip like a roasting ox.

Bardolph: Sir John, I am sure my face never hurt a hair on your head.

Falstaff: No? Look at 'em. Has it not turned 'em all grey?

Bardolph: Why, you grow old, Sir John.

Falstaff: Old! What call you old? I am a little more than threescore—and Methuselah lived near a thousand. Why may not I be a patriarch and beget sons and daughters these three hundred years myself?

Bardolph: Then you must get a wife, Sir John.

Falstaff: What to be made a cuckold of?

Bardolph: Why, Sir John, if you should marry, you would not like to be singular, I suppose.

Falstaff: Nay, for that matter, all's one. But who will have me? Your dames of breeding are too fine and finicky for me to bear with them.

Bardolph: Or they to bear with you.

Falstaff, by William Shakespeare *et al.*

Falstaff: Whoever has me must be no tenderling—I must have a kicksey-wicksey of more substantial stuff. But if she should turn out a shrew, the Lord have mercy on me. I shall be paid for the sins of my youth.

Bardolph: What think you of Dame Quickly or Doll Tearsheet?

Falstaff: I have often promised to marry 'em both. That's reason enough not to. Let me think. I have, it is true, small hopes from Hal— It is but going to Purgatory a few years before my time.

(Doll and Quickly have fallen to blows. Bardolph and Falstaff follow them out trying to separate them, with expostulations of "Ladies, Ladies, Gentlewomen." From another door, enter the Chief Justice and Pleadwell.)

Chief Justice: Are you still of that opinion? If so, my money's gone.

Pleadwell: Indeed I am still of that opinion, my Lord Chief Justice.

Chief Justice: What—how—that my money's gone?

Pleadwell: You are an attorney yourself. You should have taken a bond or obligation at the time of lending it. A thousand pounds on the bare word of a courtier—

Chief Justice: I know it well. But when the old King died, there was no time. Had I but waited one day— But is there no method in law to recover it? Can I not arrest him?

Pleadwell: Has not the King already stated he is to be at liberty? As for the debt, should he deny it, how will you prove it? And who knows on such an emergency what Sir John will not do?

Chief Justice: He'll lie—that's certain.

Pleadwell: Most consummately, too.

Chief Justice: I can prove his receipt of the money.

Pleadwell: But the conditions, my Lord Chief Justice, the conditions. What have you to shew that he is engaged to return it, and if so, when?

Chief Justice: Nothing. I was weak enough in my terror to lend it to him on his bare word.

Pleadwell: Let us speak him fair and persuade him if possible to sign an obligation for the money. If we can do that, we may trounce him.

(Enter Sir John)

Falstaff: Never, never, again will I venture my life to prevent two women from brawling. I was never in more danger of my life, not even at Shrewsbury. (seeing the Lord Chief Justice and Pleadwell) Consulting with a lawyer? Are ye thereabouts, I will go back out. (starts to steal off)

Chief Justice: Sir John, Sir John, a word with you.

Falstaff: Ah, my dear friend the Lord Chief Justice.

Pleadwell: Sir John, my lord here has—

Falstaff, by William Shakespeare *et al.*

Falstaff: Ha, mine old acquaintance, Master Wheedlepoint? How is your health, Master Wheedlepoint?

Pleadwell: Pleadwell is my name, Sir John.

Falstaff: I cry you mercy. Roundabout Pleadwell, I think. And what has become of your young partner, Harry Puzzlecase?

Pleadwell: Dead, Sir John.

Falstaff: So young?

Pleadwell: Sixty-two, Sir John.

Falstaff: Why, no older than me. To be cut off in the bud— And Dick Silvertongue. Young Dick was a devil with the women—he and the Lord Chief Justice.

Pleadwell: Dead, too. No matter, Sir John, at the present we would confer on other business.

Falstaff: Gentlemen, if you are on business, I crave your pardon and leave ye. I am not used to be impertinent.

Pleadwell: You are not going, Sir John—it is with you my business lies.

Falstaff: Business with me!

Chief Justice: Yes, with you.

Falstaff: I never do business on the Sabbath.

Pleadwell: About the thousand pounds, Sir John.

FALSTAFF, BY WILLIAM SHAKESPEARE *ET AL.*

Falstaff: What mean you, Mr. Pleadwell?

Pleadwell: Money that you borrowed of the Lord Chief Justice.

Falstaff: Take me with ye, gentlemen, let me understand ye. The Lord Chief Justice hearing that my Hal was King and not knowing what a changeling he was soon to prove presented me with a thousand pounds to promote his interest at court—or shall we say to prevent Hal from taking a just revenge for the wrong you put upon him. Depend upon it, if I can serve you, I will.

Chief Justice: Fiddle faddle, Sir John, I expect my money again. Your interest at court is not worth a farthing.

Falstaff: I cannot help that. The more is my misfortune. When you gave the money, your interest was not worth a farthing. Times change. I would have helped you if I could. You see my heart is good.

Pleadwell: If so, Sir John, you will not refuse to give his honor something to shew for his money under your hand.

Falstaff: How do you know that, Mr. Pleadwell? I must consult my counsel.

Pleadwell: No need, Sir John. I will draw up a little instrument to which you will set you hand immediately.

Falstaff: Not while I have a head. By St. Falstaff's day, I may bethink me.

Pleadwell: I know of no saint of thy family in the calendar, Sir John.

Falstaff, by William Shakespeare *et al.*

Falstaff: Well, there may be saints of a worse. But I cannot tarry now—

Pleadwell: If you will sign the instrument we will attend you—

Falstaff: Will you so? I am going to a notorious bawdy house.

Chief Justice: No matter, Sir John.

Falstaff: No matter, say you? Is it then no matter for the personification of royal authority to be seen in a public bawdy house? Why, this is as bad as if the King himself were come. Lord, Lord, what will this world come to. My conscience is more tender. I should be sorry to give occasion for scandal to the King, considering all I have given to the Prince.

Pleadwell: Please you, Sir John, be serious. Let us rightly understand each other.

Falstaff: With all my heart. To be plain with you—you do not know me. You talk to me of restitution and conditions— Did you ever know Sir John Falstaff to make restitution or conditions? Do you think me so unpracticed a courtier as to return the perquisites of my calling because I am turned out, or to restore the purchase of my good will because I am not likely to be able to use it? Rest you content: your money is in good hands, and if I do not spend it like a gentleman, why never trust me with a thousand pounds again.

Chief Justice: Don't belie me, Sir John,—don't cheat me of my money and laugh at me, too.

Falstaff, by William Shakespeare *et al.*

Pleadwell: If you had either honor or honesty, you would restore the money—

Falstaff: What, a politician and honest?

Pleadwell: As you have pretensions to neither, I leave you.

(Exit Pleadwell)

Falstaff: Will you have dinner with me?—if you will you shall see the money fairly spent and you shall share with me while it lasts. But for dry restitution—I have not been accustomed to it for many years— You would not have me be a changeling at my advanced age, I hope?

Chief Justice: Changeling! No, Sir John—but depend upon it, I will neither eat or drink with you—if the law will not help me, I will take another method.

Falstaff: Look ye, sir. You offered a bribe, d'ye see, a bribe to me. To influence the King. You were dishonest enough to give it, and I was dishonest enough to take it. That's high treason and corruption. You cannot aver the debt unless you have a mind to hang. Now, both of us having proven dishonest—why should you think me honest enough to give it back?

Chief Justice: Well I know it. But I will have my money. Depend upon it! I will have my money. I shall find a means, never fear.

(Exit the Lord Chief Justice in a rage)

Falstaff: What would that blade of spearmint have to do

with me? I have done with him.

Chief Justice: (reentering) But I have not yet done with you, Sir John. I will have my thousand pounds again.

Falstaff: You would, my lord—like enough. You must take me in the humor, I am at present ill disposed to your suit.

Chief Justice: Tut, Sir John, I have said I will not tamely put up with this wrong. If I do, I shall be flouted and jibed to death.

Falstaff: Not unlikely. But believe me, the more you bustle in this business, the more you will expose yourself. The more you stir—you know the proverb. It is a little homely, so let that pass. Yet let me advise you—rest content.

Chief Justice: No, I will not rest content. Give me back my money or I will have satisfaction.

Falstaff: Satisfaction, you say? Why, you will not dare me to combat?

Chief Justice: Such provocation would make a coward fight, Sir John. I will not put it up. By heavens, I will not put it up.

Falstaff: Well said, I see there's mettle in you. But surely you would not break the peace—you whose office it is to punish the breach of it?

Chief Justice: Sir John, there are times and reasons for all things. If you will neither give me the money, nor a gentleman's satisfaction, I will have you tossed in a blanket.

Falstaff: They must be stout carls that toss me in a blanket.

Chief Justice: We shall see, we shall see. I'll parley with you no longer. (gives Falstaff note and exits)

Falstaff: A challenge!! By the lord it is a challenge! In the name of common sense is the old fool turned into a madman? Does he think by running me through to be my heir at law? But let me see—I have it— (calling) Bardolph!

(Enter Bardolph)

Bardolph: Sir.

Falstaff: Bardolph, I have just received a challenge from the Lord Chief Justice.

Bardolph: That's ridiculous; he cannot fight.

Falstaff: I agree. It is beneath my dignity to meet him. A renowned warrior like myself against a skinny, starved civil servant. Ha, ha, ha.

Bardolph: Indeed, Sir John.

Falstaff: By the laws of chivalry, you being my squire, this quarrel is properly thine, Bardolph. You must meet him at single rapier.

Bardolph: (astonished) I, Sir John! He has no quarrel with me. The challenge is given to your honor.

Falstaff: True, but my honor disdains to fight such a pitiful, underfed creature. You must take my sword and fight him. He knows nothing of the sword. Should he challenge you at pistols present you nose to him; he'll never stand thy fire.

Bardolph: Indeed, I shall only disgrace your arms, Sir John.

Falstaff: Bardolph, you are a coward. But no matter, you have always been one. I will meet him myself. I have an idea. We will go to that magician—

Bardolph: What magician—

Falstaff: The one that can make you shot free.

Bardolph: Oh, that one. A good idea, Sir John—

BLACKOUT

Scene 4

A wizard's apartment. The area is hung with astrological charts and phenomena, possibly a skeleton or two. It is very dark.

Enter Hal, Poins, Nym, and Pistol.

Hal: (dressed as a magician) My spirits appear!! You, Nym, Pistol, Poins, when I strike my foot must enter like demons and offer to seize Falstaff. Now hide, he comes.

(Nym, Poins, and Pistol withdraw)

FALSTAFF, BY WILLIAM SHAKESPEARE *ET AL.*

(Enter Falstaff led by Bardolph)

Falstaff: Would Hal were with me: I smell so much salt-peter and brimstone that I must be near the habitation of the Devil. If I had not paid the money in advance I would not venture. Is there no way back? 'Sblood, all the doors are locked.

(Bardolph withdraws)

Hal: (rising up suddenly like the magician) Halt!

Falstaff: Quarter, quarter, I beseech you.

Hal: Approach mortal. Here are spirits of the air, others of the Stygian lake. Those are gay, and bright and fair. These than Hell itself more dark.

Falstaff: By heavens, a poetical conjuror. What would I give to answer him in his own dialect?

Hal: Mortal, why keepest thou aloof! Come hither before the fiends catch thee by the breech and drag thee to Hell.

Falstaff: Great master, I did not come to speak with thee, but with the famed Mandevil. I beg thee now to protect me from the fiends. I hear too plainly they are coming.

Hal: I am Mandevil. Set thee in that chair.

Falstaff: (quaking) A thousand thanks to great Mandevil. But you must drag me hither for I have such a load of sulfur in my mouth that my limbs are not able to bear me.

Falstaff, by William Shakespeare *et al.*

Hal: (staggering under Falstaff's weight succeeds in putting him in the chair. He then draws a circle around it.) While in the chair and in this circle, the fiends cannot hurt you. But if you stir out of it, your death be upon your own head.

Falstaff: May I not shake in it without danger?

Hal: Yes, but be sure you let not your teeth chatter. It enrages the fiends.

Falstaff: Pray for a gag, then, for fear of the worst.

Hal: Think not the worst of yourself for the disorder you are in—better men had been frightened by the devil. You desire to be invulnerable, sir. From what weapon, sword or gun?

Falstaff: Both.

Hal: But you have paid me only for one, and I have prepared accordingly—choose.

Falstaff: Let me be shot-free.

Hal: Good. Sit firm, and start not at whatever you see or hear. Beware of chattering.

Falstaff: Give me a gag.

Hal: I would not have so mean a thing done to a gentleman.

Falstaff: (holding his thumbs under his chops and biting his ruff or a handkerchief) Best act myself.

Falstaff, by William Shakespeare *et al*.

Hal: Spirits of the deep appear and inchaunt this mortal from shot by gun. Let neither pistol nor cannon have the power to make his flesh less juicy. Let his skin be tough as wall And resist the leaden ball. (he stamps his foot and three goblins appear screeching)

Falstaff: God save us.

Demon: He names a name abhorrent to us.

2nd Demon: The mortal's teeth chatter.

3rd Demon: I can't stand that noise.

Falstaff: Hal, Hal, what will I not do for you, you young sinner.

1st Demon: Pull him apart.

2nd Demon: Drag the guts to Hell.

Hal: Hold—hold—spirits. Obey your master.

(The spirits retreat)

How do your teeth chatter?

Falstaff: No, no—'tis but my bones smiting one against the other which makes a noise somewhat like it. I have kept my teeth as close as a dead man's that have been set a week. No, not my teeth. (his teeth chatter again)

Hal: Infernal spirits that delight to lie, begone. But first apply the charm.

Demons: The charm is done. Mortal be free from shot or

gun.

(Demons circle around Falstaff, hiss, clap him on the back, then suddenly exit)

Falstaff: (after a moment) Are they gone?

Hal: Yes.

Falstaff: The Devil go with them, for I do not think a gun could fright me half so much.

Hal: Oh, sir, a gun is as terrible as a demon.

Falstaff: Why, I tell you, Sir, I have had many a gun leveled at me, yet my teeth did not chatter.

Hal: Then they chattered now?

Falstaff: Give the devils their due, they were right: never did my grinders move more nimbly. It was a veritable tooth quake. Do you not think me a brave man to outface the Devil in a lie?

Hal: While your teeth were chattering too?

Falstaff: By Jove, judge what I might do when I am not in a fright, that could achieve so bold a thing when in one.

Hal: Well, you are charmed against shot, fight whom you will.

Falstaff: But how do I know I am shot-free? Though you are a famous man I should be a fool to take your bare word for it when my life, and what's more precious— my reputation are at stake.

Falstaff, by William Shakespeare *et al.*

Hal: If you will not believe me, believe you own eyes. Come, sir, here's a pistol. I'll instantly charge and show you by experiment.

Falstaff: On whom will you make this experiment?

Hal: On you.

Falstaff: On me?

Hal: My life on it.

Falstaff: 'Twill be my life on it then.

Hal: Why, you know I should be hanged if I kill you.

Falstaff: How shall I know that if I am killed? Besides, for aught I know, you have made yourself halter proof.

Hal: (having got the pistol ready) Come, sir, don't doubt. I'll soon let you see your error.

Falstaff: (ineffectually trying to dodge) Hold, hold, Cannot you give me another charm to make me fear proof?

Hal: Away with such scruples. Take the pistol and shoot me. I am charmed with the same spell.

Falstaff: This is by much the better way of trying. Have at you, sir.

Hal: I stand firm as a bastion.

Falstaff: But stay! What if I should kill you? Would I not hang?

Hal: If you be questioned say I am a suicide. No one can contradict you.

Falstaff: It's worth a white lie to be satisfied in so needful a point. Have at you.

(Falstaff shoots. Hal lets fall a ball at his foot, which he then picks up and shows to Falstaff.)

Hal: Here's the bullet and I am well.

Falstaff: Great master of Sorcery, thou modern Merlin—I beg your pardon for my doubts—and I now go to fight with firearms with any from sixteen to sixty. I'll enlist again. Whoever my fury does provoke, Shall find his destiny in fire and smoke.

(Exit strutting)

Hal: If he were as well charmed as he is fooled he would be invulnerable indeed.

BLACKOUT

Scene 5

A fencing school. Pistol and Nym are the masters. [This scene may be omitted in presentation.]

Pistol: Is this not better than the service mean of Cappadocian or Assyrian knight? How much gave that last young student?

Nym: Two marks—

Pistol: We do well.

(Enter the Chief Justice)

Chief Justice: Your servant, gentlemen. Is Signor Stilletto to be spoken with?

Pistol: The valiant wight translated is to Heaven.

Chief Justice: Ha, sorry!

Pistol: Sayst thou so, Paphlagonial vile? Wouldst thou he in Tartarus should howl? (draws) Ha—Sa!

Chief Justice: Not I, not I. Pray moderate your passion. Sir, understand me. Signor Stilletto was my honored fencing master. I had a friendship for him—

Pistol: Then I embrace thee with a soldier's arm. Stilletto was the glory of the sword, the Ajax, Hector, Agamemnon, he!

Chief Justice: And who are you?

Pistol: Men call me Sir Antich Pistolo. Do you need my service?

Chief Justice: To say the truth, sir, though I am not of a quarrelsome disposition, I have an affair of honor on my hand and not having used my sword lately would take a lesson or two.

Pistol: (to Nym) Hand the foils.

(Nym does so)

Falstaff, by William Shakespeare *et al.*

There, grasp it well.

(They skirmish, the Chief Justice falls)

Chief Justice: Enough, enough, for once, brave sir. I see your worship is a master. I'll try my skill again another time.

Nym: (aside to Pistol) Is not this the Lord Chief Justice?

Pistol: I think it is.

Nym: This will be rare sport.

Pistol: Let's break his head.

Chief Justice: (giving money) Sir, there's my thanks.

Pistol: Do not go, sir.

Chief Justice: But I must.

Pistol: I say you shall not.

Chief Justice: What?

Pistol: I like you so well, Sir, that I would give you a free lesson.

Chief Justice: Enough for one day.

Pistol: Not by half.

Chief Justice: I'd rather not.

Pistol: Handle your sword, sir, or I'll run you through.

Falstaff, by William Shakespeare *et al.*

BLACKOUT

Scene 6

The tavern. Hal and Poins dressed as monks.

Hal: Adjust your habit, Poins. There, good friar, thou hast it. Now for a lean ascetic monk.

Poins: (making a sign of the cross awkwardly) I could never get this right.

Hal: Practice. Practice. Falstaff must not know us. It would little conduce to raise the King's wisdom in the general estimation of the world to have it thought he associates with such an unworthy knight as Falstaff— Yet, so contradictory is public opinion, that it would be censured if His Highness should now act towards the said unworthy knight with an ill timed severity. That argues an ungrateful nature. I have already been censured for dismissing him so curtly at the coronation. Therefore, my Lord Chief Justice had been ordered to retract his ill-timed warrants. That's policy.

Poins: Son, well and piously observed. In the name of the Church I commend your lordship on his prudence in treating vices as infirmities.

Hal: Try to get him to retire to a monastery.

Poins: I fear my mission will prove as fruitless as that of many other apostles sent to preach to the infidels. As there is no danger of martyrdom, I am content. Persuade Jack Falstaff to turn monk—I could work miracles indeed!

Falstaff, by William Shakespeare *et al.*

Hal: But consider the richness of the jest. Mark that, Poins. It is a royal jest, is it not?

Poins: The best I ever heard if it should take.

(Enter a Page)

Page: Mistress Ford insisted that I bring her to Your Majesty, even here. I dared not refuse.

Hal: You did well.

(The Page exits)

What does she here? She would spoil the jest.

Poins: Shall I leave you, Your Majesty?

Hal: No. She is grown importunate of late.

(Enter Mrs. Ford)

Mrs. Ford: My darling, Harry.

Hal: My dear Meg—

(She embraces him. Hal is uncomfortable.)

Hal: Not here. You must not know me in public.

Mrs. Ford: Pish. Cannot the King have a mistress?

Hal: But your reputation—

Mrs. Ford: I came because I have such wonderful news—

Falstaff, by William Shakespeare *et al*.

Hal: What is it?

Mrs. Ford: My husband—

Hal: Don't mention him—

Mrs. Ford: Never again.

Hal: Eh?

Mrs. Ford: He's dead, Harry—

Hal: Dead?

Mrs. Ford: He was stabbed at the coronation—

Hal: This is strange—

Mrs. Ford: Now, nothing can stand between us— There's a spirit whispers to me: be an empress wench, a queen or a duchess. For my ambition is to advance to greatness.

Hal: (thoughtfully) Aye, that's so, Meg.

Mrs. Ford: I might be queen if you would be but a man—

Hal: Hmmm.

Mrs. Ford: And our child might be a prince. I had forgot to tell you, Harry, I am with child. He will be a boy, I'm sure.

Hal: So, so. Poins a word with you. (whispers in Poins' ear)

(Quickly and Doll Tearsheet fight their way across the stage with epithets such as "whore," "drab," and "ugly face.")

BLACKOUT

(While Hal confers with Poins, Meg preens)

Hal: Meg, I am expecting Falstaff; I have a trick to play on him that will not be equaled. Go, I will come to you later.

Mrs. Ford: Not equal to the one I played, I wager. Come soon. (she goes out)

Hal: This calls for all my diplomacy, Poins.

Poins: Would the rogue were here.

(Enter Falstaff)

Poins: Peace be with you, Sir John. God save ye.

Falstaff: Thank you, good father.

Poins: Thank you, I think thou dost not know me, Sir John—it is many years since our personal intimacy—your life and mine—

Falstaff: Were something different, father—to be sure. And though I may have seen you, it is so long since I have been to church that I must crave your pardon if I have totally forgot you. And yet your reverence may be my ghostly father for ought I know—

Falstaff, by William Shakespeare *et al.*

Poins: Fie, fie, Sir John, a man of your age and gravity.

Falstaff: Hah, if your business be to chide me, I shut my ears.

Poins: If you will not admit your wound to be probed, how can you expect to be cured, Sir John?

Falstaff: Cured! 'Sblood, I took you for a priest, not a surgeon.

Poins: A spiritual one, such as your disorder requires.

Falstaff: I am not given over by the surgeon's bodily yet. Why, call in the spiritual doctors till the earthly ones give over.

Poins: I know your case well. It is, perhaps, less your body than your mind that is affected.

Falstaff: Like enough. I have been damnably dispirited since the King's coronation—ungrateful puppy. A confounded melancholy hangs on me—

Poins: It is that melancholy and the cause of it, I would remove.

Falstaff: How? Can you provide me with a troop of horse, and restore me to the King's favor? I know no other way.

Poins: By inducing thee to repent and be restored to the favor of the King of Kings. Are you not in a state of sin?

Falstaff: By what authority do you catechize me? Do you

come out of charity or are you employed by your superiors?

Poins: Suppose the former, Sir John.

Falstaff: Why, suppose the Devil is strong in me, and I am tempted to throw you headlong downstairs for your impertinent zeal.

Poins: Your ill manners would be inexcusable were they not the consequence of your antipathy to anything that is good.—I am come by order of His Majesty, who is much interested in your reformation.

Falstaff: That's another matter. I cry you mercy, reverend father, you are not the man I took you for. What's he over there?

Poins: He is a novice under a vow of silence. He is my aide.

Falstaff: Well, well, so he is safe. Proceed.

Poins: You'll hear me then, Sir John?

Falstaff: Heaven forbid, I should not.

Poins: I am not so forward as to pry into a conscience that will not bear looking into. We know your failings.

Falstaff: There, friar, you win my heart. Come, sit down, will you drink a glass of sherry?

Poins: It is not my custom, Sir John.

Falstaff: I cry you mercy, again. Here's your health. Now,

Falstaff, by William Shakespeare *et al.*

I sit me on the stool of repentance—I have been deliberating for some time past to change my course of life. I am heartily tired of whoring and drinking.

Poins: I am glad to find you in such a promising disposition. You could do nothing more agreeable to His Majesty's intentions than to take yourself to a secluded monastery—where, separated from the temptations, and with spiritual assistance you may learn to mortify the flesh.

(Aside) I shall burst to see him stare so.

Falstaff: Hold you there, good father. Let me understand you. Hal would make a monk of me?

Poins: Exactly. Though I think you unfit myself.

Falstaff: Thank you for that! Mortify the flesh! Consider what a mortification that must be to a man who has six times the quantity of other men! If he would make a clergyman of me, could he not at least make me Archbishop of Canterbury? Canterbury is a pleasant town. Something might be said for that. But for a monk! I know not anything I am less fit for unless he had meant to make me a chimney sweep, or a running footman.

Poins: His Majesty will not use compulsion on your inclinations—

Falstaff: Oh, if I am inclined that way, depend upon it. I shall be as ready as ever to follow my inclinations.

Poins: Some steps, however, Sir John, you must take towards a more reputable life, and that speedily, too; otherwise you will be stripped of the honors of knighthood and the King's sentence of banishment will be strictly put into execution against you.

Falstaff: Hmm. Once a knight, always a knight. The King may make as many knights as he pleases but he will not so easily unmake them again. No matter for that. I am very desirous of giving His Majesty satisfaction. Only how?

Poins: Perhaps there is a way, Sir John. Marriage is a holy state. If you were to marry a widow of the King's choosing—

Falstaff: A commendable penance. An act that has confined many a man to a state of penitence to the last hour of his life.

Poins: It will insure that your penitence is not transitory owing to your late disappointment.

Falstaff: I doubt not but I shall repent me sufficiently afterwards. A pity it cannot be celebrated in prison—for marriage is a bond, therefore no fitter place to perform it. Well, well. I suppose His Majesty has chosen some drab of the parish for me.

Poins: Not so, Sir John. A wealthy widow.

Falstaff: Indeed. This sounds better. Not Mrs. Quickly? For I know he does favor that foolish woman.

Poins: No, indeed. What think you to Mistress Meg Ford?

Falstaff: A likely wench, and one enamored of me. But she had a plaguey jealous husband, and quite alive, I believe.

Poins: Her husband was stabbed to death during the coronation festivities.

Falstaff: Do you say so? I must comfort the poor soul.

Poins: Is such a marriage agreeable?

Falstaff: (cagily) I can think of no reason the King would propose such a match unless he were interested in the wench? How long has she been his mistress?

Poins: These two years. He visited her as one Master Brook. It is very secret.

Falstaff: Ah, yes. Hal was always a discreet lad. Fancy, his having a wench for two years, and I not know one word of it. The boy is deep. He'll make a real statesman. And so the King would favor me with his princess. Hot love is soon cold.

Poins: That breath were better kept to cool your porridge.

Falstaff: Could not Hal find someone fitter to marry his drab? Why not Poins? A born cuckold.

(Poins is pained, Hal smothers a chuckle.)

Poins: Poins is too close to the King. Rumors have already started that her husband died by her design so that she might marry the King and make her child blood royal.

Falstaff: I am not sure I care for this preferment. I have avoided cuckoldom these sixty years.

Poins: An awful scandal is brewing and must be prevented. The rumors must be squelched.

Falstaff: At what price?

Poins: He who renders the King this service will stand high in His Majesty's favor.

Falstaff: So he wear his horns quietly.

Poins: Amen. You are particularly suited to this task because it is known you have courted her. Without a doubt, Sir John, there are those think you capable of slipping a knife into Master Ford so you could be easy with his wife.

Falstaff: Hmm. Ten thousand pounds down—and an earldom when I am married.

Poins: What?

Falstaff: Tush, that's nothing. I do it only as a favor to Hal. If you prate, I shall insist on being a Duke.

(Hal makes vigorous signs to Poins to accept Falstaff's terms.)

BLACKOUT

SCENE 7

A field. Enter Falstaff.

Falstaff: This must be the spot, but where is the adversary?

Falstaff, by William Shakespeare *et al.*

Chief Justice: Here I am, Sir John.

Falstaff: Come, Sir John, draw, draw.

Falstaff: It calls me by my name, too! What art thou, fairy, ghost, hobgoblin or demon? Exorciso te, Pater noster—

Chief Justice: Come, Sir John, leave fooling. Don't think to put me from my purpose. You know me well enough. And you shall know me to your cost.

Falstaff: Can this be the Lord Chief Justice? I took ye for some strolling ghost of a starved man.

Chief Justice: Mocking shall not suffice you.

Falstaff: True, as I am a sinner.

Chief Justice: Will you fight or not?

Falstaff: Fight! When you see the princely eagle descend to encounter the Tom-tit. What, shall the lofty elephant wield his wild proboscis against a mite? Shall Sir John Falstaff draw his mighty sword against such a pig widgeon as you?

Chief Justice: Lay down your target and draw.

Falstaff: Who would be the fool then? If I fight it must be on equal terms— It is but equitable my body should be secured when I engage with an unsubstantial form of a thing that has none. Do you think me such a goosecap as to lay open this fair belly to the point of your rapier when you present not but a shadow for me? It were indeed a miracle to hit what is impalpable. Come, if you must fight, you shall not say I deal unfairly with you. To draw my sword is needless for hit you, I shall never—that's flat. Therefore, Toledo, rest in thy scabbard. (stands on defense with his shield) Carry the point as best you can. If you cannot come into me before you are weary, the money is mine. If you do, and wound me—I will keep it to pay the surgeon. So come on.

Chief Justice: Sir John, you are a cowardly knave, and I will kill you if I can.

(They fight. Falstaff blocks all his thrusts with his target. Hal, Poins, Nym, Pistol, Bardolph, Mrs. Ford, Quickly, and Doll appear as spectators.)

Falstaff: Well said! Bravo! To it! Again— Sa! Sa!

(The Chief Justice breaks his sword. Falstaff closes with him and seizes him by the collar.)

Falstaff: Thus does might triumph over justice. Have I nabbed you? What if I cut your throat now?

Chief Justice: My life is in your hands. But you know you have wronged me.

Falstaff: Well then, your wrongs be forgotten. On that condition I give you back your forfeited life.

Chief Justice: I hope you won't bear malice.

Falstaff: Me, malice! It is a thing foreign to my character. Why you are the very mirror of knight errantry. Nay, I will take Majesty upon me and knight you myself, "Rise up, Sir Robert Shallow, knight of the most horrible order of combatants and murderers of the fifth button."

FALSTAFF, BY WILLIAM SHAKESPEARE *ET AL*.

Why, I could marry thee to my sister.

Chief Justice: Say you so? I am but recently widowed.

(All the others applaud Falstaff)

Hal: What, at combats, my Lord Chief Justice? I thought you did not approve of subjects breaking the peace?

Chief Justice: Your Majesty, I am justly rebuked.

Falstaff: (to Mrs. Ford) Well, my fair princess, see your wandering knight.

Mrs. Ford: Welcome, Sir John. You are a wanderer and a swimmer, too.

Falstaff: A true knight errant for your sake.

Mrs. Ford: For my sake, Sir John?

Falstaff: Ay, for yours, my Helen. Have I not encountered tremendous giants and fiery dragons in the rebels of Northumberland and Wales? And then for magicians and enchanted castles; Owen Glendower and his Welsh devils—and many a stronghold have I visited releasing fair damsels from captivity and distress. I brought two of the latter to town. Would they were safely immured in the country again.

Mrs. Ford: And all these exploits for me, Sir John?

Falstaff: As I am a true knight, to lay my laurels at thy feet.

Mrs. Ford: Do you love me in sincerity, Sir John?

Falstaff, by William Shakespeare *et al.*

Falstaff: (aside) As much as you deserve, depend upon it.

(Aloud) Am I a soldier? Have I courage? Love thee! I will be thy Troilus, and thou shalt be my Cressida.

(Aside) Belike, I will play old Pandarus to thy Cressida.

Mrs. Ford: Do you swear it?

Falstaff: Can I lie? You shall be the sole possessor of me. You shall share in the honors done me at court when Hal, when His Majesty makes me an Earl. But what shall we not do? We shall be incontinently happy.

Mrs. Ford: For decency's sake I cannot well consent. I am too recently a widow. No, I will not.

(turns away)

(Hal goes to her and they quarrel silently; she still shaking her head)

Falstaff: For decency's sake there must not be too much delay.

Quickly: Sir John, is it true you are to marry this woman?

Falstaff: By royal command.

Quickly: (bawling) But you promised to marry me.

Falstaff: I'll do better. I'll pay my bill.

Doll: I forbid you to marry her. If you marry her I'll tear your eyes out.

FALSTAFF, BY WILLIAM SHAKESPEARE *ET AL*.

Falstaff: Peace, Doll, peace.

Doll: I will not peace. (pointing to Hal) There is your bride's lover. Why stand you there like a mute? Are you fascinated with your success, or are you ruminating on the comforts of cuckoldom by anticipation?

Falstaff: Away termagant jade or I will demolish your frippery. Hsst, Doll. Apply yourself to my Lord Chief Justice—I will tell him you are my sister, a widow.

Doll: Say you so? (preening) Then I'm content to wish you joy.

(She approaches the Lord Chief Justice and coquettes; he is taken with her.)

Mrs. Ford: I will not marry him.

Hal: You must.

Mrs. Ford: I will not.

(Hal moves off toward Falstaff in anger)

Hal: She says she won't do it.

Falstaff: Let me say a word to her Hal. I am experienced with your willful women.

Hal: (shrugging) Good luck.

Falstaff: What, my Helen, skittish?

Mrs. Ford: Away, you tun belly rogue.

Falstaff, by William Shakespeare *et al*.

Falstaff: What troubles my darling?

Mrs. Ford: Not your darling neither.

Falstaff: Look not upon my grey hairs. I am not so old but I can kiss thee into action.

Mrs. Ford: (thinking) Hmmph.

Falstaff: Ah, you begin to balance me.

Mrs. Ford: I do indeed, sir.

Falstaff: And how do you find me?

Mrs. Ford: Full weight, sir. Let me ask you one civil question: are you entire and sound in all your parts?

Falstaff: To tell the truth I've had a spice of the pox.

Mrs. Ford: I don't ask you about disease, but whether you have all your parts?

Falstaff: Faith, I've lost a joint or two.

Mrs. Ford: But the one proper to a husband?

Falstaff: Never fear that, wench, Do you think the King would send me to the wars without my weapons?

Mrs. Ford: Are you not too old to tilt?

Falstaff: Old in experience and most given to lechery—to tell the truth I am somewhat goatishly inclined.

Falstaff, by William Shakespeare *et al.*

Mrs. Ford: Oh, monstrous!

Falstaff: Hark in your ear, lass. (he whispers)

Mrs. Ford: And can you do that? Fie, Sir John, you'll make me blush.

Falstaff: Tush, you like it above anything in the world. But do not blush, you'll spoil your painting.

Mrs. Ford: You will not upbraid me with the Prince?

Falstaff: It is but an hour's loss of thee. I pray thee, make no more scruple of it than other women. Is it a match?

Mrs. Ford: Yes. My hand on it. This is like to be a perfect marriage for a woman.

Falstaff: Indeed, I am like to prove the most understanding husband in Christendom, and be royally rewarded for my goodness.

Hal: (coming forward) I wish you joy, Earl.

Falstaff: Thanks, Hal.

Hal: I am appointing you ambassador to the Great Turk— a land where I understand men of your great merit are well appreciated.

Falstaff: I do invite you all to supper with me. And if you cannot laugh at the success of your own contrivance, be merry at the consummation of my nuptials. For I am the first man to be cuckold the very instant he was married.

Hal: Say grace, Jack.

Falstaff, by William Shakespeare *et al.*

Falstaff: Attend me now, whilst I say grace: For salt and bread, for grapes and malt, for flesh and fish, and every dish, for mutton and beef, for cheeses and chitterlings, for tripe and fowl—and other meat that's in the house—for breasts, for legs, for loins,

(Aside) and pretty wenches,

(Aloud) for pies with raisins, for fritters, pancakes, and venison patties, for mince pies, and garlic, for butter and mustard, for wafers, spiced cakes, tart, and custard, for capons, rabbits, pigs, and geese, for apples, and pumpkins, for all these and more—Benedicamus Domino.

CURTAIN

Falstaff, by William Shakespeare *et al.*

EPILOGUE

Hal: I know you all, and will awhile uphold the unyoked humor of your idleness. Yet herein will I imitate the Sun who doth permit the base contagious clouds to smother his beauty from the world that when he please again to be himself being wanted, he may more be wondered at by breaking through the foul and ugly mists. So when this loose behavior I throw off my reformation glittering o'er my fault shall show more goodly and attract more eyes than that which hath no foil to set it off. I'll so offend to make offense a skill; reforming time when men think least I will.

Falstaff: Shit. The world is given to lying, Hal. And so, good night.

CURTAIN

FALSTAFF, BY WILLIAM SHAKESPEARE *ET AL.*

ABOUT FRANK J. MORLOCK

FRANK J. MORLOCK has written and translated many plays since retiring from the legal profession in 1992. His translations have also appeared on Project Gutenberg, the Alexandre Dumas Père web page, Literature in the Age of Napoléon, Infinite Artistries.com, and Munsey's (formerly Blackmask). In 2006 he received an award from the North American Jules Verne Society for his translations of Verne's plays. He lives and works in Maryland and México.

www.ingramcontent.com/pod-product-compliance
Lightning Source LLC
LaVergne TN
LVHW041622070426
835507LV00008B/409